REJOICING

STANLEY MOSS

Rejoicing

NEW AND COLLECTED POEMS

ANVIL PRESS POETRY

Published in 2009
by Anvil Press Poetry Ltd
Neptune House 70 Royal Hill London SE10 8RF
www.anvilpresspoetry.com

This book is published with financial assistance
from Arts Council England

Designed and set in Monotype Bembo by Anvil
Printed and bound in Great Britain
by Hobbs the Printers Ltd

ISBN 978 0 85646 417 1

A catalogue record for this book
is available from the British Library

Jane

ACKNOWLEDGMENTS

The American Poetry Review, Best American Poems of 2003, Dissent, Exile, Exquisite Corpse, The Forward, The Kentucky Review, The Nation, The New Republic, The New York Times, The New Yorker, Open City, Parnassus, Partisan Review, Pequod, PN Review (UK), *Poetry, Poetry International, Poetry London, Princeton University Library Chronicle, Shabdaguchha, Shirim, Tikkun, The Times Literary Supplement, Verse, The Virginia Quarterly.*

CONTENTS

I · *Rejoicing*

2 · Poems from *A History of Color*

3 · Poems from *Asleep in the Garden*
    and *The Intelligence of Clouds*

4 · Poems from *Skull of Adam* and *The Wrong Angel*

With exceptions for reasons of entertainment and matter, these poems are arranged in reverse chronological order.

S. M.

I
Rejoicing

The wilderness and the solitary place shall be glad for them; and the desert shall rejoice, and blossom as the rose.

ISAIAH 35:1

REJOICING

God washed his womb in the ocean.
All things that lived in or above the sea
rejoiced that they were there.
The sand under the rocks,
the driftwood trees rejoiced.
The living, those who called to their kind,
the lucky ones, rejoiced.

When I was young and prodigal,
I dived into God's womb and the ocean.
God spoke to me as I swam
through a thousand reflections,
his face and my face touched
like Mary's cheek on the cheek of her deposed son.
God washed across my face. My face was in him.
From time to time I spat him out as I swam.

I came out of his womb dripping. I felt clean.
I knew God was cold and wet wilderness.
Shivering, I dried God off me with a towel
then I hung him on a clothesline to dry.
God and the towel seemed happy and laughing,
flapping in the wind without commandments.
From the shore I could see the horizon:
he was washing his womb in the ocean
after a day of love, before his gala night.

THE BATHERS

1

In the great bronze tub of summer,
with the lions' heads cast on each side,
couples come and bathe together: each touches only
his or her lover, as he or she falls back
into the warm eucalyptus-scented waters.
It is a hot summer evening and the last
sunlight clings to the lighter and darker blues
of grapes and to the white and rose plate
on the bare marble table. Now the lovers
plunge, surface, drift—an intruding elder
would not know if there were six or two,
or be aware of the entering and withdrawing.
There is a sudden stillness of water,
the bathers whisper in the classical manner,
intimate distant things. They are forgetful
that the darkness called night is always present,
sunlight is the guest. It is the moment
of departure. They dress, by mistake exchange
some of their clothing, and linger
in the glaring night traffic of the old city.

2

I hosed down the tub after five hundred years
of lovemaking, and my few summers.
I did not know the touch of naked bodies
would give to bronze a fragile gold patina,
or that women in love jump in their lovers' tubs.
God of tubs, take pity on solitary bathers
who scrub their flesh with rough stone
and have nothing to show for bathing
but cleanliness and disillusion.

Some believe the Gods come as swans,
showers of gold, themselves, or not at all.
I think they come as bathers: lovers,
whales fountaining, hippopotami
squatting in the mud.

SONG OF ALPHABETS

When I see Arabic headlines
like the wings of snakebirds,
Persian or Chinese notices
for the arrivals and departures of buses—
information beautiful as flights of starlings,
I cannot tell vowel from consonant,
the signs of the vulnerability of the flesh
from signs for laws and government.

The Hebrew writing on the wall
is all consonants, the vowel
the ache and joy of life
is known by heart. There are words
written in my blood I cannot read.
I can believe a cloud gave us the laws,
parted the Red Sea, gave us the flood,
the rainbow. A cloud teaches kindness,
be prepared for the worst wind, be light of spirit.
Perhaps I have seen His cloud,
an ordinary mongrel cloud
that assumes nothing, demonstrates nothing,
that comforts as a dog sleeping in the room,
a presence offering not salvation
but a little peace.

My hand has touched the ancient Mayan God
whose face is words: a limestone beasthead
of flora, serpent and numbers,
the sockets of a skull I thought were vowels.
Hurrah for English, hidden miracles,
the A and E of waking and sleeping,
the O of mouth.

Thank you, Sir, alone with your name,
for the erect L in love and open-legged V,
beautiful the Tree of Words in the forest
beside the Tree of Souls, lucky the bird
that held Alpha or Omega in his beak.

RANSOM

Death is not Prime Minister or resplendent,
not eternal darkness, silence, or heaven-sent.
Death is an unrepresentative form of government,
a dead mother and father who rule without consent,
a drone in every flower, the Queen in her hive.
They have a room in every house, pay no rent.
Silent at dinner, they deceive, connive,
as the clock ticks. They never say, "Live and let live."

How many times have I tried to sing them to sleep?
Eternal bride and bridegroom,
I do what I do to make my death handsome,
to make them proud, to win a faceless smile by a leaping
somersault to childhood. I pay ransom
to my kidnappers who tie me to their bed—to weep
in their pillow, to sleep, to dream, to do or undo,
to *twinkle twinkle* in their firmament of two.

Silly to think there was a death: a father and mother
before there was time. Perhaps there was a single egg,
like the egg that hatched love, or something profane, other,
an indebtedness to which we should not pray, but beg
for more time. Or do we take a steel shovel and dig,
dig up a God, a Father who had a Holy Mother.
Perhaps love and death were married beneath a single egg,
a sign of resurrection like the butterfly.
Mothers and fathers live until their children die.

CLOUDS

Two beautiful women in the sky kissing,
their arms and legs wrapped around each other,
one has wings, is an angel. Her lover's left hand
is deep in her feathers. Her lover's right hand
reaches deep inside her. Their tongues
are pink, gentle, rough, or hard.
The miracle is that a cloud can kiss,
that if one cloud has wings and is wrapped
around the other, the other is helpless.
Now they are rolling over each other.
I wish I could carve 'Stanley'
on the white marble bluff. I am in Cardiff.
I sleep at the Angel Hotel.

A BLIND FISHERMAN

I teach my friend, a fisherman gone blind, to cast
true left, right or center and how far
between lily pads and the fallen cedar.
Darkness is precious, how long will darkness last?
Our bait, worms, have no professors, they live
in darkness, can be taught fear of light.
Cut into threes even sixes they live
separate lives, recoil from light.
He tells me, "I am seldom blind
when I dream, morning is anthracite,
I play blind man's bluff,
I cannot find myself,
my shoe, the sink,
tell time, but that's spilled milk and ink,
the lost and found I cannot find.
I can tell the difference between a mollusk and a whelk,
a grieving liar and a lemon rind."
Laughing, he says, "I still hope the worm will turn,
pink, lank, and warm, dined
out on apples of good fortune.
Books have a faintly legible smell.
Divorced from the sun, I am a kind
of bachelor henpecked by the night.
Sometimes I use my darkness well—
in the overcast and sunlight of my mind.
I can still wink, sing, my eyes are songs."
Darkness is precious, how long will darkness last?
He could not fish, he could not walk, he fell
in his own feces. He wept. He died where he fell.
The power of beauty to right all wrongs
is hard for me to sell.

SONG OF NO GOD

With any luck you can still find a rain god
in a cornfield, chaotic symmetry, a sacred wood,
although nothing remains of certain gods
but an octagonal vault and part of a leg. Enough.
The moon goddess doesn't weep, the sun god does not laugh.
I strike a match to light the night, a puff
of smoke, no more. I strike another to light the day
to prove I do not need a sun god anyway.
The No God inside me is not a golden calf.
My No God has two dogs: Night and Day.
They take their time, they do not come to me.
I whistle, call "stay, stay." They do what they rather.
"I'll take you in the car to run along the sea."
They race what is, what was and what will be.
They take their time and sniff an apple tree
because there in moonlight the deer gather
to eat apples and praise their heavenly father.
I pray weary of his nothingness my No God
will not call back his dogs: Night and Day,
or, for his pleasure, let slip another flood.

HERMAPHRODITES IN THE GARDEN

I

After the lesson of the serpent there is the lesson
of the slug and the snail—hermaphrodites,
they prosper on or under leaves, green or dead,
perhaps within the flower. See how slowly
on a windless day the clouds move over the garden
while the slug and the snail, little by little, pursue
their kind. Each pair with four sexes
knows to whom it belongs, as a horse knows
where each of its four feet is on a narrow path:
two straight below the eyes, two a length behind.
There is cause and reason for,
but in the garden, mostly life befalls.
Each male female lies with a male female,
folds and unfolds, enters and withdraws.
On some seventh day after a seventh day they rest,
too plural for narratives, or dreams, or parables,
after their season. One by one they simply die—
in no special order each sex leaves the other
without comfort or desire.

2

I open my hands of shadow and shell that covered my face—
they offered little protection from shame or the world.
I return to the garden, time's mash of flowers,
stigmas and anthers in sunlight and fragrant rain.
Human, singular, the slug of my tongue
moves from crevice to crevice, while my ear,
distant cousin of a snail, follows the breathing
and pink trillium of a woman who is beautiful
as the garden is beautiful, beyond joy and sorrow,
where every part of every flower is joy and sorrow.

I, lost in beauty, cannot tell which is which,
the body's fragrant symmetry from its rhymes.
I am surrounded by your moist providence.
A red and purple sunrise blinds me.

GLUTTON

If I could I'd gorge on Time, twirl hours on my fork
and wipe my plate clean with my daily bread,
but I am Time's pretzel, his pistachio nut.
I wish I were Time's spaghetti carbonara.
I am what he munches, kept on the bar
long enough for the waitress to take the order,
for Time to be seated whoever he is—
this godlike No God who little by little
devours me. Eat, eat, my Lord,
you will not swallow me in one gulp.
I will give you such indigestion in Paradise
with my hard head, stiff neck, broken bones,
you will wish you were never born. Eat.
You may think, Wise Guy, you can fart me out,
but what about Mount Etna, Vesuvius,
who were those nobodies?
Invisible universal glutton,
lift your little trident! Keep me off your plate!
Eat your sheep, not this Jew.

THE CELLIST

To Daniel Stern

You cherished your silent beautiful cello
after your shoulder joint wore out.
You would not play dead like that entombed Jew.
You could not stop hearing music in your head:
a disease. Whatever the conversation
or dream, you hear the chamber music you played—
the Archduke Trio, concerti in your head
in the Monday, Tuesday, everyday world—
the first cousin of a religious experience.
Sometimes I ask: "What music is playing now?"
The evening program, however sublime, always seems painful.
You sold your cello to pay a doctor's bill.
It could have happened in a Balzac story—
wherever you are, outside in the street Balzac is standing,
winter and summer, fat and naked beneath his bronze cloak.

We are hanging on to life by a cello string.
I take the A string that carries the lyric, you the G
for darkness and light, both holding on to Dear life,
to D for Darling, Divertimento, and Don't let go.
Our C string sounds at the bottom of a well.
The Great Concertmaster is playing us
for the hell of it. We are his cello.
His bow the tails of a hundred white horses.
Maestro, keep playing, an aire on any string will do,
Mozart, Bach, jazz, a little street music.
Sing us or pluck a note from time to time,
or a chord with one turn of the wrist
to accommodate the curve of the bridge.
Practice, practice, practice. O Concertmaster,
a question we, the cello, ask with our undersong
of lust: "Do we love the world more than one person?"
—again with a turn of the wrist
to accommodate the bridge over the dark river.

POETS AT LUNCH

To W. S. Merwin

I said, "Nothing for the last time."
You said, "Everything for the last time."
Later I thought you made everything more
precious with "everything for the last time":
the last meditation, the last falling asleep,
the last dream before the final makebelieve,
the last kiss good night,
the last look out the window at the last moonlight.
Last leaves no time to hesitate.
I would drink strong coffee before my last sleep.
I'd rather remember childhood, rehearse forgiveness,
listen to birdsong or a Spanish housemaid singing,
scrubbing a tiled floor in Seville—
I'd scrub and sing myself. *O Susanna*
Susanna, quanta pena mi costi.
I would strangle the snakes of lastness
like Herakles in his crib
before I cocked my ear to Mozart for the last time.
There is not sky or clouds enough to cover
the music I would hear for the last time.
I know a bank whereon the wild thyme of
everything for the last time grows, covered with
deadly nightshade and poison hemlock.

No last, no first, thinking in the moment,
years ago, you prepared the soil in Hawaii
before you planted your palm trees, then shared
most of your days and nights with them as equals.
You built your house with a Zen room.
I made no prayer when I dug a hole
and pushed in a twelve-foot white pine,
root ball locked in green plastic netting.

I did not cut the netting, so twenty years later
a tall, beautiful, white pine died.
I lynched the roots. To save my life
I would let them seize, cut out a bear's heart,
I would partake in its flesh.
But you would die before you'd let them kill that bear.
Again, I say, "Nothing for the last time."
You say, "Everything for the last time."
Sailor, I would have killed a stranger
to save the world. Sailor, you would not.
We kissed goodbye on the cheek.
I hope not for the last time.

Home, I look into my brass telescope—
at the far end, where the moon and distant stars
should be, I see my eye looking back at me,
it's twinkling and winking like a star. I go to bed.
My dogs, donkeys and wife are sleeping. I am safe.
You are home with your wife
you met and decided to marry in four days.

AN AMERICAN HERO

It wasn't all smell of Adirondack lilac
and flowering chestnut trees along Broadway
in the spring of 1824.
Human sewers, mostly Negroes, carried waste in tubs
at night to the Hudson and East Rivers. James Hewlett,
said to be ex-slave, ex-tubman, self-purchaser,
ex-houseboy to English actors, leapt up like a wildcat,
then like a witch, he joined a Shakespeare theater of ex-slaves,
billed himself: "Vocalist and Shakespeare's Proud Representative."
I pick his pocket.
He played Richard the Third and Othello,
sang *Il Barbiere*, *La Marseillaise*, and "O!
say not that woman's love is bought" in one evening.
Humped in silk, Mr. Hewlett called out:
"Now is the winter of our discontent
made glorious summer by this son of New York,"
to black applause. Whatever the beauty of the season,
his actors and actresses were beaten up,
his theater finally burned to the speechless ground.

I pick his pocket.

Adrift in an open boat, he let the winds of eloquence
take him where they would. Often, late at night, he recited
speeches from Shakespeare in the street,
sometimes in the snow.
In disgrace for marrying a pretty-as-a-picture white woman,
he served six months for stealing wine, then three years
for stealing a silver watch from the vest pocket
of a dead man, a show off laid out in tails.
What good is a watch in the grave?
He answered the sentencing with
"I have done the state some service, and they know it."
I pick his pocket.

While he was away playing with himself,
better people attended the fashionable theater
and minstrel shows, danced the cotillion. The industrious poor—
slaves who bought their freedom, or whose fathers or mothers
had bought their freedom, a few simply freed—
dressed up as no one had dressed before, hired ballrooms,
danced the cotillion too, held a benefit dance and supper
to support Greek freedom. Late in the evening,
sweating and full of whiskey, their loins sweetened,
they fell to what whites called "crazy dancing
and senseless music" that "frightened the horses."

Out, Hewlett gave one last performance, a newspaper reported:
"to great applause he made a fine speech before the curtain,
which ended up—he could not help himself—
in some kind of talk you had to be a nigger to understand."
I pick his pocket.

Signed up on a crew of freemen and slaves
he made his way to Trinidad,
"Shakespeare's Proud Representative" found a stage,
portrayed Mr. Keene playing nine tragic roles.
Sometimes he gave himself laughing gas to please the crowd
or pretended to. A one-man band,
Othello sang *La Marseillaise*. I pick his pocket.

He disappeared in New York in the forties,
the streets slave-free after 1827,
full of Negroes and Irish; older, there is no reason to think
he was kidnapped and shipped south for sale.

What had it come to beyond the gaslights
and wood fires? History as entertainment,
a stained purse I grab. I sit in the dark, listening
to a call and response, a call and response.
For no reason, beauty reports, disappears

not like early-morning birdsong in the city
but like the report of a rifle. I pick his pocket
in the third balcony of my life; segregated from myself,
I am barely a ghost in my own poem.

OVER DRINKS

The day is a lion across the horizon,
the forests, a thorn in its foot,
it gnaws on hapless years, its stomach full.
The lion rolls on its back kicking the heavens.
The lion of Judah is part of its pride, its mate—
some say the favorite.

Furthest from the truth: the night, the universe
is a black Labrador pup biting
as if we were its mother's teat.
Lear's fool says, "Truth's a dog, must to kennel . . ."
One day the mind will dream up an equation
for reality—I may grasp in my mouth
as a bitch holds her pup
or some, an after-dinner mint. It's true the night
is the same for the sun, the rose and us,
I mouth metaphors for memory like the zoo,
put lovers in cages with primates and reptiles.
I remember a mother sea lion feeding her young—
balancing a spinning world on the tip of her nose.
There is still time to rejoice in it all.
The Irish say, over drinks, "The night is still a pup."

SONG OF AN IMAGINARY ARAB

Until they killed my brother who killed you,
there were readers who read and smiled at:
From the rock of my heart a horse rose
that I should ride to follow them
the night they left by taxi
from the Damascus gate and fled toward Bombay.
My heart threw me off.
If only I had robes white enough,
but my robes were full of ashes and dust.
The rouge, lipstick and eyeshadows
you left on my flesh, I washed off before prayer.
My heart was gone, it looked back at me
from a distance, its reins bitten through.

Until they killed my brother who killed you,
there were readers who read and smiled at:
It is written, Muhammad was created from a blood clot.
When I am put in the grave and those who question the dead ask me,
"Was the blood drawn from the finger of God
or the heart or His tongue?"
I will not answer. I will say, "I have heard music so beautiful
it seemed the blood of the Lord."
I know there is profit in God's word, in prayer rugs, in silk and wool,
blood of the lamb and spit of the worm.
A man who rose from barber to physician,
I prize most my grandmother's brass tray, pure as the sun
without etching or design, where I first saw the angel of mathematics,
the stateless angel of astronomy.

Let an old Palestinian grandmother sit in the sun
beside an old Jewish grandmother; I'll bring them sage tea,
which in Hebrew is something like "Miriam," because when Mary
was pregnant with Jesus sage tea comforted her.
The Jew said, "Respect is more important than the Talmud."

I was admiring the girl on the balcony in Ramallah
when the shrapnel hit me in the head. I did not have time
to make the break between my thoughts
and the attack on my head.
I thought it was a flower pot that fell off the balcony.
"Allahu akhbar!" I shouted. Someday the horse will fly.

Until they killed my brother who killed you,
there were readers who read and smiled at:
Love now is more dangerous than hate.

THE WILD DOGS OF SAN MIGUEL DE ALLENDE

At the school in the Plaza Hotel, Mexico,
I taught the young and old what I could:
Learn from the starving dogs of San Miguel
how to see and listen. Do not waste a word
or a syllable, they are loaves and fishes,
enough to feed five thousand. No lies:
angels are specific, the devil generalizes.
We know there is mythological bread.
When you use what is called a metaphor
it is just an alibi, unless you knead it
like a baker kneads dough to make it rise
to bread, or cake, to—whatever, the devil's word.
Then use it. That's what you do for a living.

In the hills of San Miguel there are snakes
that once were walking sticks. Saint Hubert
was converted when he saw a stag
with a crucifix between its antlers.
Who has not seen a starving dog in headlights
running with a crucifix in its mouth?
At night when the wind dies down, some who listen
hear the Virgin weeping. She knows starving dogs
at the foot of the cross, snarling at evil,
licked up her son's pooling blood while He suffered,
and after, when she held Him, licked His wounds.

Any dog can nose a rat in the anus of the rich,
mercy in the asshole of the poor. Red-haired
Judas fed his good dog under the table.
The starving dogs of San Miguel de Allende
will carry off your sorrows if you put your trust in them,
or feed them from your hand.
Easier to speak for wild dogs than the poor.

WILDFLOWERS

What sweet company they were for an hour or night.
Yes, I kissed them, but I left them after
my crude human lying down and getting up.
I learned their purpose: their being and beauty
is entirely erotic, but that is not to know them.
I never entered them deeper than sunlight,
never ravished their petals and perfumes.
Their pollens were wasted on me.
Socrates said, "My knowledge such as it is
is nothing but a knowledge of erotic things."
Athenian, rest in your marble dust.
In the rummage and agora of my life,
on this summer evening my day is done,
the Lord is not a botanist
who art in heaven. He does not lead me
into green pastures. He is already there
delivering me from evil. Dandelions and false dandelions,
I am completely unprincipled, I lie with you
disobedient to the laws of cities.

VANITAS

In the sideview mirror of my car
through the morning fog I saw a human skull
that had to be my face, where the headlights
of the car behind me should have been,
or a morning star. I did not think
to step on the gas and race away from the skull
I knew wasn't behind me. Still it had me by the throat.
I can tell a raven from a crow,
a female evergreen from a male,
but I can't tell visionary bone from ghost.
I'm used to my eyes fibbing to me,
5s are sometimes 8s, 2s, 3s.
I know the Chinese character for the word "nature"
is a nose that stands for breathing—life.
I need to see an ancient nose in the mirror.

ANONYMOUS POET

Sometimes I would see her with her lovers
walking through the Village, the wind
strapped about her ankles.
Simply being, she fought
against the enemies of love and poetry
like Achilles in wrath.
Her tongue was not a lake,
but it lifted her lovers
with the gentle strength of a lake
that lifts a cove of waterlilies—
her blue eyes, the sky above them—
till night fell and the mysteries began.
My friend I love, poet I love,
if you are not reading or writing tonight
on your Underwood typewriter,
if no one is kissing you, death is real.

THE UNICORN

Here is a lady with a unicorn in her lap,
a holy mother with a unicorn,
a symbol of Christ the Savior,
a black horse with a yellow horn and yellow tail.
I see the Lady with a unicorn, a savior who is not Christ,
but poetry. She kisses the beast
who licks her face. The unicorn
pokes its horn in her neck, a sign of love,
closes its eyes, falls asleep in her arms,
forgets all suffering.

In a heartbeat, heart beating so hard
you can hear it, the beast awakens,
runs about the house, kissing books and sharpening its horn,
today on free forms. Rising on its back legs
it stands on Shakespeare—
showing its golden penis, it ejaculates,
then grazes in "the valley of its saying,"
on Góngora, Lorca, the Psalms,
washing and feeding the poorest of the poor,
until, with the excuse that it is in love,
or loveless, it returns to the barn, the library—
weeping because it is only a metaphor,
captured in the lap of the virgin.

ON BEES DISAPPEARING IN AMERICA
AND EUROPE BUT NOT IN BRITAIN

Someone is playing tricks on flowers and blossoming trees;
now you see, now you don't see bees, wasps and hornets.
This summer, the hives and nests are empty,
pollen and nectar dry untouched, unsucked in the cup.
Perhaps gunsmoke and lies did them in.
Bees are royalists, perhaps a little democracy
did them in. I can tell a bumblebee from a hummingbird,
how Samson found bees in a lion's carcass.
I remember Psalm 118:
The nations compassed me about like bees;
they are quenched as the fire of thorns:
for in the name of the Lord I will destroy them.
—a passage St. Augustine read as referring to Christ's capture.
Yes, I am grateful for the gift of black ants
to peonies, the sexy winds of summer, while insecticides
stop and question butterflies who lost their memory
in fields and gardens of America.
Hail Britannia, where queens and drones still prosper,
kept alive, I think, in public and private gardens
by Shakespeare in the air.

GODMOTHERS

In my family the identical twin sisters
Mercy and Womb were named after words
in the Hebrew Bible spelled alike.
What luck to have two aunts,
godmothers, who kissed me on the mouth,
wished me well cautiously when I did wrong—
when I tried to right myself it was not
to disappoint them. They weren't religious, just loving.
I ached to hear them say, "There, there,"
while they held me close, my Womb, my Mercy.

On the crazy side of my family,
I had a distant cousin who got the electric chair.
They never forgave themselves.
How many times did I hear them say,
"If you wrong someone only he or she can forgive you,
not God." Mercy walked the picket lines against injustice
until her feet bled, Womb was an agitator.
If ever you hear a note of Womb or Mercy
in my voice, it is because something of those twins,
those darling girls and beautiful women,
those immigrants, lives in me.

FOR MY GODMOTHER, TWENTY YEARS LATER

Give me a death like hers without tears,
those flies on a summer day about a carcass—
about the house medicine, Mozart, and good cheer.
My song: life is short, art long, death longer.
My doctor uncle covered her with kisses.
When her life was a goldfinch in his hand,
on a feeder and birdbath outside her window:
larks sang, splashed and fed above the sparrows.
A blue jay militaire drove them away.
Then, a bird of prey, a necessary reprimand
screamed overhead without mercy. Instead
of terror, it was met at her window
by the warbler of good cheer that sometimes sings for the dead.
I whistle for it to come and nest near my window.

EL SOL

If *the sun is money*, as you say,
the ocean has deep pockets.
Three miles down there's still a little flickering,
small change in the deep—eight miles further
the sun is broke, flat as a flounder.
In Lima it rains once a year;
people are hot and tired of too much money.
While in sunny Spain anarchists in the Civil War
made leaves money. *Duros* and *pesetas* were out.
Olive trees cashed in.
Your typical wallet *portafoglio* held oak leaves,
olive leaves, and laurel. On rare occasions
a newspaper photo of Lorca was found
among the leaves. (Some things never change:
Cuentos verdes are still dirty jokes,
Judias, Jewish women, *Judias verdes*, green beans.)
When anarchists burned the churches,
if caught they sometimes confessed to the priests
before they were shot against a sunrise of money.
Would to Allah leaves were still money,
paintings of Adam with money over his privates.
In 1909 anarchists protesting conscription to Africa
dug nuns from their graves and danced
with those money-covered nuns in the streets of Barcelona.
The sun is the root of all evil. Sun talks.
Blake pointed out, some see the sun as a golden guinea.
He saw it as the heavenly host crying, *holy, holy, holy*.

TSUNAMI SONG

A father is teaching his daughter to swim
in the Indian Ocean,
near them a fisherman throws his net,
silver and pink fish leap out of reach,
the child, wearing water wings,
loves her accomplishment,
squeals and laughs.
The father is happy teaching his daughter
something useful that will give her joy
the rest of her life. He says, "Come to me."
When the great stone ocean falls from the sky,
for a second, the rest of her life,
the child thinks she is swimming—
then she is a pebble in the deep.
The father, reaching for his daughter,
disappears, a shard of blue glass.
Like a seagull the water wings fly
to the foot of the mountain.
Despite a broken wing
it tries to rise from the sand.

I walk along the North Atlantic
with my wife and two dogs.
A horseshoe crab writes in the sand,
the sun disappears,
everything darkness with no one to see it,
the moon a skull in the sky.

THE RING IN MY NOSE

A Birthday Card for Hans Magnus Enzensberger

There is a woman in all living things, a lily.
A wounded soldier dying is a woman dying in childbirth,
a dead black soldier may be the black woman
who gave birth after she was lynched.
My mother at eighty-three died singing lullabies.
For her sake, half in mourning, half in farce,
I put her wedding ring through my nose,
tied it on a string attached to a cloud
that pulls me south down the Hudson,
noses me over industrial parks,
east over Long Island suburbs once home.
A loving pig is yanked over the pine barrens,
past Shinnecock, Conscience Point, then adrift
over the shipless Atlantic. Who or what
holds the string? Father, mother, or some
old cloudy hatred? It cannot be a butterfly
that pulls me out of reason—
perhaps some phantom pain, or pleasure, lifts me to bed,
or from cloud to cloud, beyond birthdays,
till I am over China, where woman is half the sky.

PEACE

The trade of war is over, there are no more battles,
but simple murder is still in.
The No God, Time, creeps his way,
universe after universe, like a great snapping turtle
opening its mouth wagging its tongue
to look like a worm or leech
so deceived hungry fish, every living thing
swims in to feed. Quarks long for dark holes,
atoms butter up molecules, protons do unto neutrons
what they would have neutrons do unto them.
The trade of war has been over so long,
the meaning of war in the O.E.D. is now "nonsense."
In the Russian Efron Encyclopedia,
war, *voina*, means "dog shit";
in the Littré, *guerre* is "a verse form, obsolete";
in Germany, *Krieg* has become "a whipped-cream pastry";
Sea of Words, the Chinese dictionary,
has war, *zhan zheng*, as "making love in public,"
while war in Arabic and Hebrew, with the same
Semitic throat, *harb* and *milchamah*, is defined
as "anything our distant grandfathers ate
we no longer find tempting—like the eyes of sheep."
And lions eat grass.

BAD JOKE

After a difficult illness, in letters to friends I wrote:
"Inside my vitals it was Stalingrad."
I could have said "Waterloo, all puns intended."
I never would have said "a holocaust inside my belly."
Only God could have the holocaust in His belly,
or, on second thought, Stalingrad inside His belly
with a million five hundred thousand dead,
among them battalions of Russian women,
everyday Russians and everyday Germans
in with the slaughtered *Wehrmacht* and Panzer
divisions—a few well-disciplined innocents
"On the wrong side of history" and the Volga:
Romanians, Hungarians, the Spanish Blue Division.
They say the Lord passes days and nights on battlefields,
although I doubt he spends his time by human measure.
In His belly they were starved, frozen, gassed,
shot to death, blown to pieces,
or done in by subtler vehicles of departure.
God does not digest or belch. Yesterday, His time,
He devoured men battling with stone axes and clubs,
He downed all history and our yesterday's dead.
Are His eyes on fire without tears?
Does He evacuate? The perfect being never makes a stink.
War is the hair on His head,
the beard He strokes when He sits in judgment.
He would never have a little fat belly like Buddha.
Looking around the world, I say to God,
"Careful, you may just fall on your face."
And so I move to farce.

LISTENING TO WATER

Water wanted to live.
It went to the sun,
came back laughing.
Water wanted to live.
It went to a tree
struck by lightning.
It came back laughing.
It went to blood. It went to womb.
It washed the face of every living thing.
A touch of it came to death, a mold.
A touch of it was sexual, brought life to death.
It was Jubal, inventor of music,
the flute and the lyre.

"Listen to waters," my teacher said,
"then play the slow movement
of Schubert's late sonata in A,
it must sound like the first bird
that sang in the world."

AUTUMN

For Stanley Kunitz

In a dream after he died
I received picture postcards
from him every day for two weeks
in a single night—the picture:
blazing maples and walnut trees,
New England in full foliage.
I wept that he should write
to me and my wife in a handwriting not his
in blue ink so often.
Since I do not remember the text,
I suppose the message was:
"Every autumn you know where to find me."

HOTEL ROOM BIRTHDAY PARTY, FLORENCE

Mirror, mirror on the wall,
who's that old guy in my room?
In the red nightshirt on my bed
I'm a kabuki extra. If I please
I can marry all
to nothing, snow to maple trees,
leap for joy over my head,
play bride and bridegroom,
an old and young shadow on the wall.
I can play a decapitated head
laughing in its basket of flies.
There are no clocks in paradise,
a dog's tail keeps time instead.
(Today be foolish for my sake.)
Which comes last, sunset or sunrise?
Nightfall or daybreak?
The day is Puccini's,
the street is for madrigals
the celebration in the cathedral:
a skull beside a loaf of bread,
but for my grandmother's sake
it's a portion of *torta di nonna*★ I take.
It is a double portion of everything I want.

A mirror is a stage: I'm all the comedies
of my father's house and one of the tragedies.
I draw my boyhood face
in blood and charcoal
I hold my masks in place—
all the worse for wear
with a little spit behind the ear,

★ *grandmother's cake*

53

and because this is my birthday
like a donkey in its stall
let fall what may.
To be alive is not everything
but it is a very good beginning.

THE ICEHOUSE AND THE POND

1

Winter. The ice slept here, the father ice
with his eye sharp as ice-tongs, that cold anger
under sawdust, never thanking
the wind or a cloud over the sun
for a little relief from the pain of being ice,
while the blue-eyed ice, whose breast he sucked for coldness,
crashed into the logs that shored up the roof.
Still what shade there was came from her
who loved the snow truly, the long below-zero nights
after a snowfall that were God-given.

2

A child looked out at the pond,
the frogs, and dry cattails,
a broken oar still iced in.
Peer deep as he could through the ice
he only saw white, silver, violet, black;
there was the red gill of a fish on a nail
near the roof, but that was as rare as laughter
in the icehouse.
The flowers on the hillside confused him
especially the mouth-red flames.

Despite crosscut saws, ice-tongs and axes,
he made his way over the frozen straw,
through the abandoned snake nest,
toward the forbidden windows, doors, slides.
He melted ever so slowly.
He was disobedient,
though in his heart he knew he was one of them
and always would be, there was nothing

that could change him under the sun
as he slipped out between the floorboards,
down the hillside.
He made his way to the red flowers, he was sure
it was his love for them that washed
him into the brook—he loved the stones,
the roots of trees, the trout swimming through him
and leaping for flies, the ferns and webs barely
touched his cheek. Part of a brook,
these days he looks back at the icehouse.
He remembers the first dank lesson:
the joy of receiving gifts being ice-picked
out of him. Old ice, palsied now.
Someone killed a water moccasin,
threw half an orange on its head.
He knows his gifts, counts his blessings.
It had become possible
for any living thing to consume him.

3

Summer. When I swim in the pond that is language
I am at best a tourist with an American accent.
I swim into deep water. I can't touch bottom.
I think grammar is down there in the mud.
I can dive down in the icy water
touch something unborn
among the egg layers and live bearers,
the imperfect, the pluperfect,
pollywogs of words.
I swim, which signals I am not a floating oar.
Take your frog, leech, turtle, fishkind,
I devour, reproduce, live for pleasure with them.
Unlike the clouds, we are earthlings, we swimmers
the Yets, the Stills, the Howevers
half-asleep in the sun,

afraid of our kind. I make for shallow
water. I kiss waterlilies.
I think they kiss back, an old story.
God's womb holds on to my foot.
I am deep, shallow, and muddy,
I look back over my shoulder,
remember the icehouse and the warm belly of a rabbit.

GRACE

In the great iron pot of the universe
there is *pot-au-feu* for dinner:
gravity, galaxies, darkness, plasma;
my host, my dearest and least dear father,
sits at table without conversation,
rhetoric or grammar—none I comprehend.
I am thankful for much that I swallow
and for tonight's guests: the great what is
in front of me, to my left the face of a clam,
to my right the sky brought down to its knees.
Hungry, I rush through "God is memory."
I am thankful I am not green as parsley,
I put my red and white checked napkin under my chin,
I eat with the manners of Saturn.

THEN

In our graves we become
children again
then we are grandchildren
then great-grandchildren
and so on, name after name
till we are nameless
free as the birds to sing
songs without words
mating calls, warnings
simple trills, for no reason,
that call the day is glorious.

IN THE RAIN

There are principles I would die for,
but not to worship this God or that. To live
I'd kneel before the Egyptian insect god, the dung beetle
who rolls a ball of mud or dung across the ground
as if he were moving the solar disc or host across the sky.
I would pray to a blue scarab inlaid in lapis lazuli
suggestive of the heavens.
The Lord is many. I sit writing at the feet of a baboon god
counterfeit to counterfeit. My Lord smiles, barks and scratches,
all prayers to him are the honking of geese.
To live I'd pray to a god with the head of a crocodile
and the body of a man or a woman: *our father who art in river,*
holy mother, dozing in mud, sunning thyself,
look on your young in danger, open your crocodile mouth,
the doors of your cathedral, let us all swim in.
We are gathered by the river, nesting on your tongue, swim us to safety.
Believers and unbelievers rejoice together in the rain.

THREE SONGS FOR A SINGLE STRING

I

I wish the praying wind would hire me
to help out in the valley.
In the morning when the clouds are low,
I can push clouds up toward heaven—
that Muhammad said lies under the feet
of every mother.

2

You may trick a she-camel or goat
to feed on hay stuffed in the skin of her dead kid
so she will give milk to serve her master,
or an orphaned kid or camel.
In my tradition
one of the names of God is Breast.
Almighty Breast, may I be tricked to give
the love for my dead to the living.
You will have to do more than show me
a lock of hair and a glass of whiskey.

3

The ocean, stars, mountains
without their least attention
have mated with me, as they do
with all living things.
What can I do to serve them?
Give them my bones to play with.

THE MESSIAH COMES TO VENICE

He rode into the city unrecognized on a lion,
wore a pointed hat with fool's bells,
whetting his knife on his lion's haunch. Someone shouted,
"He made the laws before he made the world."
His hand dripping oils, the rider pointed at the voice.
"I want my bond, since I made the laws before the world."
The lion bowed its head.
"Christians, Muslims, Jews, I will teach you to be content,
one as the other. Know this law:
you must first be one, then the other,
Jew play Christian and Muslim, Muslim play Jew
and Christian. Christian, wear my gabardine, then be a Turk.
That is my bond, the pound of flesh I cut from your heart.
You must learn to leave the meat of your life behind,
as an infant cut from its mother—
whatever the nothingness you call years.
Kick me, spit on me, or praise me—no matter.
I stand for judgment.
Now play your parts. Change gods, change gods,
then do the dance you call *your days*."
A lion is swimming in the Grand Canal.

2

A History of Color

God is the sole being who has no need to exist in order to reign.

BAUDELAIRE

A HISTORY OF COLOR

I

What is heaven but the history of color,
dyes washed out of laundry, cloth and cloud,
mystical rouge, lipstick, eyeshadows? Harlot nature,
explain the color of tongue, lips, nipples,
against Death, come-ons of labia, penis, the anus,
the concupiscent color wheels of insects and birds,
explain why Christian gold and blue tempt the kneeling,
why Muslim green is miraculous in the desert,
why the personification of the rainbow is Iris,
why Aphrodite, the mother of Eros, married
the god of fire, why *Adam* in Hebrew
comes out of the redness of earth . . .
The cosmos and impatiens I planted this June
may outlast me, these yellow, pink and blue annuals
do not sell indulgences, a rose ravishes a rose.
The silver and purple pollen that has blown on the roof
of my car concludes a sacred conversation.

Against Death washerwomen and philosophers
sought a fixative for colors to replace unstable substances
like saliva, urine and blood, the long process of boiling,
washing and rinsing. It is Death who works
with clean hands and a pure heart. Against him
Phoenician red-purple dyes taken from sea snails, the colors
fixed by exposing wool to air of the morning seas near Sidon,
or the sunlight and winds on the limestone cliffs of Crete—
all lost, which explains a limestone coastline
changed into mountains of pink-veined marble,
the discarded bodies of gods.
Of course Phoenician purple made for gods
and heroes cannot be produced nowadays.
Virgil thought purple was the color of the soul—

all lost. Anyone can see the arithmetic when purple
was pegged to the quantity and price of seashells.

Remember
the common gray and white seagull looked down
at the Roman Republic, at the brick red and terracotta
dominant after the pale yellow stone of the Greek world,
into the glare of the Empire's white marble.
The sapphire and onyx housefly that circled
the jeweled crowns of Byzantium buzzed prayers,
thinks what it thinks, survives. Under a Greek sky
the churches held Christ alive to supplicants,
a dove alighted on a hand torn by nails.
In holy light and darkness
the presence of Christ is cupped in gold.
Death holds, whether you believe Christ
is there before you or not, you will not see Him later—
sooner prick the night sky with a needle to find the moon.

2

I fight Death with peppermints, a sweet to recall
the Dark Ages before the word *Orange* existed.
In illuminated manuscripts St. Jerome,
his robes *egg-red*, is seen translating in the desert,
a golden lion at his feet—
or he is tied to a column naked in a dream,
flagellated for reading satires and Pliny's
Natural History that describes
the colors used by Apelles, the Greek master,
a painting of grapes so true to life
birds would alight on them to feed.
Death, you tourist, you've seen it all and better before,
your taste: whipped saints sucking chastity's thumb,
while you eat your candy of diseased and undernourished infants.

On an afternoon when death seemed no more than a newspaper
in a language I could not read, I remember
looking down at Jerusalem from the Mount of Olives,
that my friend said: "Jerusalem is a harlot,
everyone who passes leaves a gift."
Do birds of prey sing madrigals?
Outside the walls of Jerusalem, the crusaders
dumped mounts of dead Muslims
and their green banners, the severed heads of Jews,
some still wrapped in prayer shawls,
while the Christian dead sprawled near the place of a skull
which is called in Hebrew *Golgotha*.
Among the living, blood and blood-soaked prayers,
on the land of God's broken promises—a flagged javelin
stuck into the Holy Sepulcher as into a wild boar.

Hauled back by the *Franks*, colors never seen in Europe,
wonders of Islam, taffetas, organdies, brocades, damasks.
Gold-threaded cloth that seemed made for the Queen of Heaven
was copied in Italy on certain paintings of Our Lady,
on her blue robes in gold in Arabic:
"There is no God but God, Muhammad is His Prophet"—
for whom but Death to read?
Wrapped in a looted prayer rug,
an idea seized by Aquinas: the separation of faith and reason.
Later nicked from the library of Baghdad:
the invention of paper brought from China
by pilgrims on a hajj, looted rhyme, lenses,
notes on removing cataracts.
Certain veils would be lifted from the eyes of Europe,
all only for Death to see.
Within sight of Giotto's white, green and pink marble bell tower
that sounded the promise of Paradise,
plants and insects were used for dyes made from oak gall,
bastard saffron, beetle, canary weed, cockroach,
the fixative was fermented piss from a young boy

or a man drunk on red wine, while the painters
mixed their pigments with egg yolks and albumen,
gold with lime, garlic, wax and casein
that dried hard as adamantine, buffed with a polished agate
or a wolf's tooth.

At the time of the Plague, while the dead
lay unattended in the streets of Europe,
the yellow flag hung out more often than washing,
someone cloistered wrote a text
on making red from cinnabar, saffron from crocus,
each page an illumined example.
At the Last Supper the disciples sat dead at table.
Still, by the late fifteenth century
color was seen as ornament,
almost parallel to the colors of rhetoric,
blue was moving away from its place describing
the vaults of heaven to the changing sky of everyday.
Does it matter to heaven if a sleeve is blue or red or black?
In Venice Titian found adding lead-white to azurite-blue
changed a blue sleeve to satin.

     3

I think the absence of color is like a life without love.
A master can draw every passion with a pencil, but light,
shadow and dark cannot reveal the lavender iris
between the opened thighs of a girl still almost a child,
or, before life was through with her, the red and purple
pomegranate at the center of her being.

Against Death on an English day Newton discovered
a single ray of white light refracted,
decomposed into a spectrum of colors,
and that he could reconstruct the totality,
mischievously reverse the process,

then produce white light again—which perhaps is why
last century, in a painting by Max Ernst,
the Holy Mother is spanking the baby Jesus.

Goethe found a like proof on a sunny summer day—
the birds, I suppose, as usual devouring insects
courting to the last moment of life.
While sitting by a crystal pool watching
soldiers fishing for trout, the poet was taken
by spectrums of color refracted from a ceramic shard
at the bottom of the pool, then from the tails of swimming trout
catching fire and disappearing,
until a rush of thirsty horses, tired and dirtied by war,
muddied the waters.

A heroic tenor sings to the exploding sun:
"Every war is a new dawning"—Fascist music.
Death would etch Saturn devouring his children on coins,
if someone would take his money.
Of course his IOU is good as gold.

Turner had sailors lash him to the mast
to see into a storm, then he painted slavers
throwing overboard the dead and dying,
sharks swimming through shades of red.
Later he painted the atheist *Avalanche*, then heaven
in truthful colors: *Rain, Steam, Speed.*
"Portraits of nothing and very like," they said, "tinted steam."
Turner kept most of his paintings to leave to England,
his *Burning of the Houses of Parliament.*

Against oblivion a still life of two red apples
stands for a beautiful woman. On her shoulder
the bruise of a painter's brush—she is no more
than a still life of peasant shoes.
"You will not keep apples or shoes or France," Death says.

69

A child chooses an object first for color,
then for form, in rooms with mother, father,
Death, and all the relatives of being.

      4

Now this coloratura moves offstage
to the present, which is a kind of intermission.
My friend Mark Rothko painted a last canvas,
gray and yellow, then took a kitchen knife, half cut off his wrists
bound and knotted behind his back
(a trick of the mind Seneca never mastered)
to throw off Eros, who rode his back and whipped him
even after he was dead, till Eros, the little Greek,
was covered with blood of the Song of Songs.
Now Rothko is a study of color, a purple chapel,
a still river where he looks for his mother and father.

Death, you tourist with too much luggage,
you can distinguish the living from your dead.
Can you tell Poseidon's trident from a cake fork,
the living from the living,
winter from summer, autumn from spring?
In a sunless world, even bats nurse their young,
hang upside down looking for heaven,
make love in a world where the lion, afraid of no beast,
runs in terror from a white chicken. Such are your winnings.
Death, I think you take your greatest pleasure
in watching us murdering in great numbers
in ways even you have not planned.
They say in paradise every third thought is of earth
and a woman with a child at her breast.

PSALM

God of paper and writing, God of first and last drafts,
God of dislikes, God of everyday occasions—
He is not my servant, does not work for tips.
Under the dome of the Roman Pantheon,
God in three persons carries a cross on his back
as an aging centaur, hands bound behind his back, carries Eros.
Chinese God of examinations: bloodwork, biopsy,
urine analysis, grant me the grade of <u>fair</u> in the study of dark holes,
<u>fair</u> in anus, self-knowledge, and the leaves of the vagina
like the pages of a book in the vision of Ezekiel.
May I also open my mouth and read the book by eating it,
swallow its meaning. My Shepherd, let me continue to just pass
in the army of the living,
keep me from the ranks of the excellent dead.
It's true I worshiped Aphrodite
who has driven me off with her slipper
after my worst ways pleased her.
I make noise for the Lord.
My Shepherd, I want, I want, I want.

THE BLANKET

The man who never prays
accepts that the wheat field in summer
kneels in prayer when the wind blows across it,
that the wordless rain and snow
protect the world from blasphemy.
His wife covers him with a blanket
on a cold night—it is, perhaps, a prayer?
The man who never prays says kindness and prayer
are close, but not as close as sleep and death.
He does not observe the Days of Awe,
all days are equally holy to him.
In late September, he goes swimming
in the ocean, surrounded by divine intervention.

TO MY FRIEND BORN BLIND

You told me your blindness is not seeing
even the shades of black called darkness.
You felt useless as a mirror until you made a poem
useful as a dog with bells around its neck.
Sometimes you wake to the wind moving through different trees.
A child, you loved to touch your mother's face,
you wished the world were ocean,
you could hear, smell, and taste, knew that it was blue.
Trees had a smell you called green, apples red.
How could the flag be red-white-and-blue?
You laugh when I tell you "drink to me only with thine eyes"
is a love song, that some who see
only make love in the dark. You wish you could see as a bat.
Mozart you say is the great equalizer, the truest democrat,
you always preferred a dog to a cane.
When in Braille you first read, "the disciples asked,
'Rabbi, who sinned, this man or his parents, that he was born blind?'
Jesus answered, 'Neither hath this man sinned nor his parents,
but that the works of God should be revealed in him ...'
and he spat on the ground and healed the man
with his spit and mud—" you waited awhile, then read on.
Blind in dreams, you touch, taste, smell and hear—
see nothing, nightmares like crowds are the more terrible
because you never see what terrifies you.
Since childhood it was an act of faith
to believe the sun and moon were in the sky,
it pleased you the sun is a fire the sighted cannot look into . . .
It is late. As always you, my imaginary friend,
take me by the hand and lead me to bed.

HEART WORK

No moon is as precisely round as the surgeon's light
I see in the center of my heart.
Dangling in a lake of blood, a stainless steel hook,
unbaited, is fishing in my heart for clots.
Across the moon I see a familiar dragonfly,
a certain peace comes of that. Then the dragonfly
gives death or gives birth to a spider it becomes—
they are fishing in my heart with a bare hook,
without a worm—they didn't even fish like that
when the Iroquois owned Manhattan.
Shall I die looking into my heart, seeing so little,
will the table I lie on become a barge, floating
endlessly down river, or a garbage scow?

There is a storm over the lake.
There are night creatures about me:
a Chinese doctor's face I like and a raccoon I like,
I hear a woman reciting numbers growing larger and larger
which I take as bad news—I think I see a turtle,
then on the surface an asp or coral snake.
One bite from a coral snake in Mexico,
you'll take a machete and cut off your arm
if you want to live. I would do that if it would help.

I say, "It's a miracle." The Chinese doctor and the moon
look down on me, and say silently, "Who is this idiot?"
I tell myself, if I lie still enough I'll have a chance,
if I keep my eyes open they will not close forever.
I recall that Muhammad was born from a blood clot.
If I'm smiling, my smile must be like a scissors opening,
a knife is praying to a knife.
Little did I know, in a day, on a Walkman,
I would hear Mozart's second piano concerto,

that I would see a flock of Canada geese flying south
down the East River past the smokestacks of Long Island City.
I had forgotten the beauty in the world.
I remember. I remember.

ELEGY FOR THE ANCIENT TREE

That tree was a teacher, whatever the weather—
everyday birds, hawks and osprey nested
in its branches, nations of common insects
fought in its gullies, while generations of deer
scraped their antlers against its trunk in rutting season.
Looking up to its crown, it seemed higher than the Brooklyn Bridge
from a ferry passing beneath—some were frightened.
Remember the tree's gentleness with bees and butterflies,
its hospitality to rodents, lavender and Lad's-love,
that for centuries horned lizards, toads
and snakes hid in its dens—the joys and sorrows it found
in heavy rains and snows, its heroism
at the timberline, its lifelong love of clouds.
The golden-mantled squirrel survives.

Curious to take the ancient tree's measure, an "arborist"
chose to count its rings by drilling with a diamond-tipped corer.
Putting his back into the drill, as if the tree were marble,
he quickly passed through American history,
knot and counter-knot, to the age of Mozart,
through the Baroque, through Shakespearian grain,
through a charcoal cave where lightning struck,
through the time of Jesus and Buddha's enlightenment,
through the guano of owls, the Olmec.
In the era of the prophets, the drill broke—
what could a tree person do? After clearing away young trees,
to save his drill, he appealed to forest rangers.
It took five, with orange hydraulic saws, to fell the great tree.
The rings they counted came to four thousand nine hundred years.
The tree they killed was the oldest known living thing on earth.

Where can you weep for the tree that had wept and laughed
beyond all human consequence? No one could agree
what poured out: butterflies or troupes of prima ballerinas,

old men or unemployed youths who never found a purpose,
newspapers, folios, books, leaflets or turtles
with ancient Chinese writing on their backs.
A madman shouted that God had carried the tree to heaven.
Everyone let him rave. Some say the fallen tree began to shudder
and sing a requiem for all the slaughtered, innocent multitudes.
Lingering for a moment before they disappeared,
two shadows searched for their young.
Or were they two readers in the Warsaw ghetto
stopping to buy a book out of a discarded baby carriage?

THE LOST BROTHER

I knew that tree was my lost brother
when I heard he was cut down
at four thousand eight hundred sixty-two years;
I knew we had the same mother.
His death pained me. I made up a story.
I realized, when I saw his photograph,
he was an evergreen, a bristlecone like me
who had lived from an early age
with a certain amount of dieback,
at impossible locations, at elevations
over 10,000 feet in extreme weather.
His company: other conifers,
the rosy finch, the rock wren, the raven and clouds,
blue and silver insects that fed mostly off each other.
Some years bighorn sheep visited in summer—
he was entertained by red bats, black-tailed jackrabbits,
horned lizards, the creatures old and young he sheltered.
Beside him in the shade, pink mountain pennyroyal—
to his south, white angelica.
I am prepared to live as long as he did
(it would please our mother),
live with clouds and those I love
suffering with God.
Sooner or later, some bag of wind will cut me down.

SONG OF INCIVILITY

There is a place between good and evil
where lovers go to bed, kisses are not civil,
where the sun and moon are rivals
where lovers are in rapture
following their good nature.
They do not know which way is endless night,
where the heat of day, where the light of departure.
Loneliness appears at sunrise, when the naked foot
returns to earth and two hypocrites
put on the mortal boot.

SUBWAY TOKEN

If Walt Whitman were alive and young and still living in Brooklyn,
he would have seen the burning Trade Center,
and if he were old and still in Camden, New Jersey,
he would have seen men jumping out from a hundred stories up,
some holding hands, believers and nonbelievers
who prefer a leap of faith to a death in an ocean of fire.
Walt could have seen women falling from the sun,
although the sun has no offices.
True in the heavens there often has been a kind of tit for tat,
not just thunder for lightning:
where there is grandeur observed, something human, trivial.

The South Tower fell like the old Whitman,
although it was second to be struck,
then the North Tower like the young Whitman.
What history, what hallucination?
Anyone could see the towers fell like the great poet,
with three thousand people from eighty-seven countries,
and three hundred and forty-three firefighters
into the irrational fires that burned for ninety days.
None of the dead lived in a boarding house
as would be likely in Whitman's time.
History, hallucination?
A life goes up in flame like a page of Bible paper.
You could not pile books so high, not good books,
as this grand canyon of steel and concrete body parts,
my city's broken backbone pushed out through his throat.

THE GOOD SHEPHERD

Because he would not abandon the flock for a lost sheep
after the others had bedded down for the night,
he turned back, searched the thickets and gullies.
Sleepless, while the flock dozed in the morning mist
he searched the pastures up ahead. Winter nearing,
our wool heavy with brambles, ropes of muddy ice,
he did not abandon the lost sheep, even when the snows came.

Still, I knew there was only a thin line
between the good shepherd and the butcher.
How many lambs had put their heads between the shepherd's knees,
closed their eyes, offering their neck to the knife?
Familiar—the quick thuds of the club doing its work.
More than once at night I saw the halo coming.
I ran like a deer and hid among rocks,
or I crawled under a bush, my heart in thorns.

During the day I lived my life in clover
watching out for the halo.
I swore on the day the good shepherd catches hold,
trying to wrestle me to the ground and bind my feet,
I will buck like a ram and bite like a wolf,
although I taste the famous blood
I will break loose! I will race under the gates of heaven,
Back to the mortal fields, my flock, my stubbled grass and mud.

A FALL

For Stanley Kunitz

The mouth on his forehead is stitched and smiling,
his head is crowned with bandages,
his broken nose: Michelangelo's slave marble.
Like the last minutes of summer sunset
his cheekbones and eyes are lavender and black.
The face that hit the cement sidewalk of 12th Street
with the full force of his gravity does not frown.
I refuse to see what I know. I kiss the mouth of sorrow,
I rejoice that he is alive. I am drinking his gin
as if I were the English Consul,
he Lorca's gypsy nun chased by the wind.

In his sitting room that is part greenhouse
we are on the sea of poetry in a familiar squall.
I must speak louder now above the wind.
We are on the green and mountainous Atlantic,
yes, there is a "cargo of roses," a reason to smile.
Blaaah, blaaah. It is time to hold hands.
I hear the cries of poets washed overboard in my throat.
He says he is the oldest poet who ever lived,
fifteen years older than King Lear.
Now we are two old fishermen mending nets,
untying knots, hoping for fair weather—
then at sea between Emerson's "Over-soul"
and "The tear is an intellectual thing."
At Saint Vincent's I will visit his love who broke her hip.
He says, "One step closer, I would have caught her."
I will come Tuesday to cook, bring a new poem.
In his easy chair, his fist on the tiller, life is north northeast,
he heads windward, a hummingbird
blown out on the North Atlantic
struggling toward land to kiss a flower.

THE CELESTIAL FOX

1

Death is a celestial fox that leaps out of his coffin,
tonight his tail sweeps away insects,
which the religious read as a sign:
the fox kills but does not end their lives.
Sometimes he stops, noses the air,
sings, showing his teeth.
I wish I just owed him money.

2

When my two dogs and I run on the beach
innocently thinking we hunt the fox
because we see two eyes in the ocean
where the fox crouches at the foot of a great wave,
my dogs jump in barking at nothing I can see,
while the fox leaps into its true lair,
the moist den of every sexual act.
There he waits, waits with that I-told-you-so grin.

3

I am a great cunt waiting for death to fuck me
between the golden thighs of endless morning,
swaddled in labia. American,
architect of my own destiny,
he shall not flatter me or marry me,
he shall not suck me or finger fuck me
though I am wet as the Mississippi,
death shall not slip it in.

THE FALCON

My son carries my ghost on his shoulder, a falcon,
I am careful not to dig in my claws. I play
I am his father owl, sometimes sparrow, a hummingbird
in his ear. I told him from my first chirp:
"Be an American democratic Jew mensch-bird."
When he was a child in Italy I was a migrant bird
with a nest in America. When I flew home
he cried, "*Perche, perche*?" I wept
not wanting him to have a distant bird
or a sea captain for a father.
How many times did I cross the Atlantic
in the worst weather to perch outside his window?
What kind of nest could I make in Italy
on a hotel balcony? When he needed to be held
his mother and nannies took turns. When he reached out
to me he often fell. He said *I know I know* to everything
I might have taught him. I fought for his life
with one wing tied behind my back—
for his name, school, and to have his hair cut
in a man's barber shop, not a salon for signoras.
"Lose to him! Lose to him!" his mother screamed.
I was the only one in his life
who would not throw a footrace
he could win in a year, fair and square.
How could a small boy spend so much time
laughing and talking to a father in restaurants?
He complained in Bologna I took him to six museums,
in Florence four, in Espagna *mille e tre*.
We laughed at those rare Italian birds
who don't find themselves sleeping forever
on a bed of polenta—preening, displaying,
making a *bella figura*. An omen in his life.
I flew him to an English meadow

to study Dante, then Shakespeare's histories
in a king maple overlooking the Hudson,
the cast: himself, me, my mate the beautiful Jane bird.

What are years? Not a herd of cattle,
perhaps a flock of birds passing overhead.
Sometimes I hear him chirping my song
louder than I ever sang it.
One day, when the heavenly dogs and hell dogs
find me behind a bush and fight over me,
may one with a soft mouth break from the pack
and take most of me to his Master. Let Him say, "Good dog,
good dog, what a peculiar kind of bird is this,
with his gray curly feathers and strange beak?
Have I ever heard him sing?" May it dawn upon Him,
I am the bird with the good son.

CODA

DNA evidence shows all human beings have an early black African heritage.

So if God made us in His image
and likeness He's a black man.
Which did He hate more,
crucifixion or slavery?
Adam and Eve were black,
Cain and Abel black.
Somewhere there was
a white man in the woodpile.

Maybe God, come back,
had to drink at a Negro fountain—
wasn't what he meant by dividing the waters.
Black Jesus or Jehovah's voice
walked in the cool of the day.

Not that whites invented slavery,
they just made more money at it,
made it a Christian virtue,
found when they got a taste for it,
like good whiskey, watering it down a little
is better than nothing.

But God did not come back
despite His fame.
Maybe He or She is a timekeeper,
an hourglass or town clock,
a cheap wristwatch?
We are all clocks waiting to stop,
while the pigeons gather in the square below,
for better or worse.
I vote for Obama for better.

UBUNTU

I salute a word, I stand up and give it my chair,
because this one Zulu word, *ubuntu*,
holds what English takes seven to say:
"the essential dignity of every human being."
I give my hand to *ubuntu*—
the simple, everyday South African word
for the English mouthful.
I do not know the black Jerusalems of Africa,
or how to dance its sacred dances.
I can not play Christ's two commandments on the drums:
"Love God" and "Love thy neighbor as thyself."
I do not believe the spirits of the dead
are closer to God than the living,
nor do I take to my heart
the Christ-like word *ubuntu*
that teaches reconciliation
of murderers, torturers, accomplices,
with victims still living.
It is not blood but *ubuntu*
that is the manure of freedom.

BEAUTY IS NOT EASY

What are they but cattle, these butterflies,
their purple hides torn by barbed wire,
scarred blue, yellow and scarlet.
If they are not marked for slaughter
I cannot tell to whom they belong.
They are just stray cattle.
The sun does not witness,
the clouds do not testify.
Beauty does not need a public defender,
but I would listen to a serious defense
of beauty—tell me what happens to the carcass,
the choice cuts, everything useful:
hide, bones, intestines, fat.
Then talk to me of butterflies.

SONG FOR A LOST RIVER

Now there are four rivers: once there were five,
one has left without tears or a bird cry,
rivers leave their beds, have nothing else to give,
when a lover goes, love does not die—
in an empty bed love will survive.
Love, the sweet invisible spy,
is lucky: it has tears and laughter,
for a while, past, present and hereafter.

RAINBOWS AND CIRCUMCISION*

I

He might have made some other sign,
but it fitted his purpose to use sunlight
behind rain to make his sign of the covenant,
a rainbow above the flood. What was in the sky
was suddenly moral, moonlight and passing clouds
were merely beautiful.

We answer the rainbow with an infant son,
cut a touch of ignorant flesh away.
The wordless infant stands on the Book
that separates him by the width of the pages
from the bookless ground.

Rainbow and mother, tell me who I am!
We might have used another sign,
a red dot on the forehead, or a scar on the cheek,
to show the world who we are,
but our sign is intimate, for ourselves
and those who see us naked—like poetry.

2

Once in Rome, on a winter day after a rare snowfall,
I stood on a hill above the snow-covered arches,
columns and palm trees of the pillaged Forum.
Against a dark purple sky suddenly opened
by shafts of sunlight, I saw two rainbows.
To see all that at the same time, and two rainbows,
was a pagan and religious thing: holy,
it was like the thunderous beauty of a psalm, and like
peeking through the keyhole with the masturbating slaves,
watching Hector mounted on Andromache. O rainbows!

* Rainbow and circumcision: each is a biblical sign of the Covenant.

I HAVE COME TO JERUSALEM

I have come to Jerusalem
because I have a right to,
bringing my family who did not come with me,
who never thought I would bring them here.
I carry them as a sleeping child to bed.
Who of them would not forgive me?
I have come to Jerusalem to dream
I found my mother's mother by chance,
white-haired and beautiful, frightened behind a column,
in a large reception room filled with strangers
wearing overcoats. After forty-two years
I had to explain who I was. "I'm Stanley,
your grandson." We kissed and hugged and laughed,
she said we were a modern family,
one of the first to ride on trains.
I hadn't seen before how much she looked like
her great-great-granddaughter. I remembered
that in her house I thumped her piano,
I saw my first painting, a garden, by her lost son.
I remembered the smells of her bedroom:
lace-covered pillows, a face-powdered Old Testament.
Then my dead mother and father came into the room.
I showed them whom I'd found and gave everybody chocolates,
we spoke of what was new
and they called me only by my secret name.

JERUSALEM: EASTER, PASSOVER

I

The first days of April in the fields—
a congregation of nameless green,
those with delicate faces have come
and the thorn and thistle,
trees in purple bloom,
some lifting broken branches.
After a rain the true believers:
cacti surrounded by yellow flowers,
green harps and solitary scholars.
By late afternoon a nation of flowers: Taioun,
the bitter sexual smell of Israel,
with its Arabic name, the flowering red clusters
they call *Blood of the Maccabees*,
the lilies of Saint Catherine, cool to touch,
beside a tree named *The Killing Father*,
with its thin red bark of testimony.
In the sand a face of rusted iron
has two missing eyes.

2

There are not flowers enough to tell,
over heavy electronic gear
under the Arab-Israeli moon,
the words of those who see in the Dome of the Rock
a footprint of the Prophet's horse,
or hear the parallel reasoning
of King David's psalms and harp,
or touch the empty tomb.
It is beyond a wheat field to tell
Christ performed two miracles: first he rose,
and then he convinced many that he rose.

For the roadside cornflower
that is only what it is,
it is too much to answer
why the world is so, or so, or other.
It is beyond the reach
or craft of flowers to name
the plagues visited on Egypt,
or to bloom into saying why
at the Passover table Jews discard
a drop of wine for each plague, not to drink
the full glass of their enemy's suffering.
It is not enough to be carried off by the wind,
to feed the birds, and honey the bees.

3

On this bright Easter morning
smelling of Arab bread,
what if God simply changed his mind
and called out into the city,
"Thou shalt not kill," and, like an angry father,
"I will not say it another time!"
They are praying too much in Jerusalem,
reading and praying beside street fires,
too much holy bread, leavened and unleavened,
the children kick a ball of fire,
play Islamic and Jewish games:
scissors cut paper, paper covers rock, rock breaks scissors.
I catch myself almost praying
for the first time in my life,
to a God I treat like a nettle
on my trouser cuff.
Let rock build houses,
writing cover paper, scissors cut suits.

4

The wind and sunlight commingle
with the walls of Jerusalem,
are worked and reworked, are lifted up,
have spirit, are written,
while stones I pick up in the field
at random have almost no spirit,
are not written.

Is happiness a red ribbon on a white horse,
or the black Arabian stallion
I saw tethered in the courtyard of the old city?
What a relief to see someone repair
an old frying pan with a hammer,
anvil and charcoal fire, a utensil worth keeping.
God, why not keep us? Make me useful.

A GUEST IN JERUSALEM

On the grapes and oranges you gave me on a white plate: worry,
in the kitchen, day worry, in the bedroom, night worry
about a child getting killed; worry in the everyday gardens
of Jerusalem, on geraniums and roses from the time they bloom
in December, long as they live. In the desert wind
playing over the hair on a child's head and arms, worry.
In the morning you put on a soiled or clean shirt of worry,
drink its tea, eat its bread and honey. I wish you the luxury
of worrying about aging or money, instead of a child getting killed,
that no mother or father should know the sorrow
that comes when there is nothing to worry about anymore.

EXCHANGE OF GIFTS

You gave me Jerusalem marble,
gypsum from the Judean desert,
granite from the Sinai,
a collection of biblical rock.
I gave you a side of smoked salmon,
a tape of the Magic Flute—
my lox was full of history and silence,
your stones tasted of firstness
and lastness, Jewish cooking.

You took me to a synagogue where a small boy came up to me
and asked me to dance him on my shoulders.
So we danced around Genesis and the Song
of Solomon. He clapped his hands to be riding
the biggest horse in Judea. I cantered lightly
around Deuteronomy, whirled around the Psalms,
Kings and Job. I leapt into the sweaty
life-loving, Book-loving air of happiness.

Breathless I kissed the child and put him down,
but another child climbed up my back.
I danced this one around Proverbs and that one
around Exodus and Ecclesiastes, till a child came up to me
who was a fat horse himself, and I had to halt.

What could I give you after that?
—When I left, a bottle of wine, half a bottle of oil,
some tomatoes and onions, my love.

THE LOUSE

In a room overlooking Jerusalem,
I felt something like a leaf on my forehead—
I picked off a louse,
squashed it between the labyrinths
of my index finger and my thumb.
I have faith every louse in Jerusalem
has come through hair and feather:
Jew, Muslim, Christian
from wing to head to beard to crotch,
from cat's ear to rat's balls . . .
At the Jerusalem wall between Heaven and Hell
the unprepared are given skullcaps—
I refused a clean, gray paper cap,
the kind given children in different colors
at birthday parties with other favors;
I picked dusty black rayon someone left behind
despite my friend's warning: "You may get lice."
Whatever the time of day, a little before fear,
the sun hurt my eyes. I kissed the wall
but had nothing further to say to it . . .
My louse's cousins have spent time among hyena packs,
nestled in carrion, under pus, lip to lip with maggots.
Surely Christ, who suffered crucifixion,
felt the bite of the louse. My fingers are Roman soldiers
if the louse I squashed had a trace of Christ's blood.
I have faith King David after all his adventures
had an itch in the groin, and a louse danced with him.
Once a winged horse with a peacock's tail
and a woman's face flew into this city from Arabia
with a prophet on its back.
We all can use a little sacred preening and combing.
I should be grateful for another louse.

A VISIT TO KAUNAS

I put on my Mosaic horns, a pointed beard,
my goat-hoof feet—my nose, eyes, hair and ears
are just right—and walk the streets of the old ghetto.
In May under the giant lilac and blooming chestnut trees
I am the only dirty word in the Lithuanian language.
I taxi to the death camp and to the forest
where only the birds are gay, freight trains still screech,
scream and stop. I have origins here, not roots,
origins among the ashes of shoemakers
and scholars, below the roots of these Christmas trees,
and below the pits filled with charred splinters of bone
covered with fathoms of concrete. But I am the devil,
I know in the city someone wears the good gold watch
given to him by a mother to save her infant
thrown in a sewer. Someone still tells time by that watch,
I think it is the town clock.

Perhaps Lithuanian that has three words for soul
needs more words for murder—murder as bread:
"Please pass the murder and butter" gets you to:
"The wine you are drinking is my blood,
the murder you are eating is my body."
Who planted the lilac and chestnut trees?
Whose woods are these? I think I know.
I do my little devil dance,
my goat hooves click on the stone streets.
Das Lied von der Erde
ist Murder, Murder, Murder.

GHETTO THEATER, VILNIUS, 1941

Perhaps the players chose to wear something
about the person, a spoon, or since it was autumn
a large gold maple leaf that looked like a star of David
pinned to a shirt or blouse. The play was *One Can't Know Anything*.
Someone shouted: "You are play-acting in a cemetery!"
But they went on: "To sit, to stand, to lie on the ground,
is it better to close or open your eyes, to listen or not,
to speak or not to speak? Those are the questions."
Then a grave song: "I knew him well, Horatio.
Here hung the lips I have kissed I know not how often . . .
My Lord, I have some remembrances of yours."

Fifty-six years later in a sandlot where for three hundred years
the Great Synagogue stood, I watch children playing.
Perhaps God shows himself as hide and seek,
as wrestling, laughter, as children falling,
cutting their knees, and the rush of tears.

WORK SONG

As full of Christianity
as the sea of salt,
the English tongue
my mother and father spoke,
so rich in Germanic tree and God worship
and old Romantic Catholic nouns,
does not quite work for me
at family burials or other,
as we say in English,
sacramental moments.

Although I know the Pater Noster
and Stabat Mater as popular songs,
I am surprised, when close friends
speak Hebrew, that I understand nothing.
Something in me expects to understand them
without the least effort,
as a bird knows song.
There is a language of prayers unsaid
I cannot speak.
A man can count himself lucky these days to be alive,
an instrument of ten strings,
or to be gently carried off by sleep and death.

What of belief? Like the tides
there is and is not a temple of words
on which work continues.
Unsynagogued, unschooled, but lettered,
I drag a block of uncut marble—
I have seen prayers pushed
into the crevices of the West Wall,
books stacked against the boulders,
ordinary men standing beside prophets and scoundrels.
I know the great stoneworkers can show the wind in marble,
ecstasy, blood, a button left undone.

TO ARIEL, MY ARABIST FRIEND

In a museum forty years after it happened
I saw a snapshot of my lost brother,
a Hellenistic Jew, sitting in a lifeboat,
wordless, a few yards from the shoreline of Palestine,
behind him a rusty sinking freighter,
his two years in a displaced persons' camp,
his two years in Treblinka.
With him in the boat, half a dozen Jews,
tired to death and hopeful, my brother
sat in the middle, somehow a little apart,
in a good overcoat, his gloved hands
in his pockets, thumbs out, his tilted fedora
brim up, a clean handkerchief in his breast pocket
as our mother taught him, still the boulevardier,
the *flâneur*. Knee deep in the water
to meet the boat and help them in, Mr. Kraus
from Frankfurt, giving the newcomers his card,
directing them to his Viennese pastry shop,
the best in Palestine.
My brother washed more than one death
out of his handkerchief. For me as a child
his handkerchief was a white mouse
he set free in Europe's worst winter,
when it became inhuman to love.

Ariel, whose language am I speaking?

NEAR MACHPELAH/HEBRON

It was not a dream: a poet
led me down into the earth
where the sea in another age
had hollowed out a mountain.
He led me into a cave of marble cloud:
colossal backs, shoulders, thighs of reclining Gods.
Just above us a battlefield four thousand years old,
some olive trees and wild flowers.
I cannot believe these Gods need
more than an occasional lizard
or the sacrifice of a dove that comes to them
through jags and crevices.
Madness to think the Gods
are invisible, in us, and worth fighting for
—if they want anything, I suppose,
it is for the sea to come back again.

BABIES

Babies, babies,
before you can see more than light or darkness,
before your mothers have kissed your heads,
I come to you with news of dead and dying friends.
You so close to the miracle of life,
lend me a miracle to bring to my friend.
Babies, babies.
Once Death was a baby, he grasped God's little finger
to keep from falling—kicking and chortling
on his back, unbaptized, uncircumcised,
but invited to share sunlight and darkness
with the rest of us. Mother Death would nurse him,
comfort and wash him when he soiled himself
in the arms of the mourners and the heartbroken.

Older, Death took his place
at table beside his mother—her "angel."
They ate and drank from each other's mouth and fingers,
laughed at their private jokes. He could play
any musical instrument, knew all music by heart,
all birdsong, the purr, growl, snort, or whine
of each and every animal.
The story goes that, fat with eternal life,
older than his mother, he devoured her,
far from light or darkness.

Babies, at the moment of your first uncertain breath,
when your mother's magic blood is still upon you,
I come to you, the helpless ones still coughing
from miracles of birth.
Babies hardly heavier than clouds,
in desperation, for my friend, for a lark

I hold up the sac you broke through
as if it were *Saint Veronica's Veil*—
but no face is on it, no blood.
I hold up a heavy sack of useless words.
I shake a rattle to catch your eye or first smile.

PRAISE

For Yehuda Amichai

I

Snow clouds shadow the bay, on the ice the odd fallen gull.
I try to keep my friend from dying by remembering
his childhood of praise to God, who needs us all. Würzburg:
the grownups are inside saying prayers for the dead,
the children are sent out to play—their laughter
more sacred than prayer. After dark his father
blesses and kisses him *gute Nacht*. He wakes
to go to school with children who stayed behind
and were murdered before promotion.

Now his wife lies beside him.
He may die with her head on his pillow.
He sings in his sleep:
"Her breasts are white sheep that appear on the mountain,
her belly is like a heap of wheat set about with lilies."
Awake, he says, as if telling me a secret:
"When metaphor and reality come together, death occurs."
His life is a light, fresh snow blowing across the bay.

2

A year later in Jerusalem, he carries a fallen soldier
on his back, himself. The text for the day begins:
"He slew a lion in the pit in a time of snow."
Seconds, minutes, hours are flesh,
he tells me he is being cut to pieces—
if they had not made him turn in his rifle . . .
He sees I cannot bear more of that.
Yet a little sleep, a little slumber, a little folding
of hands in sleep and we drink to *life*.

105

Chilled in desert heat, what keeps him alive:
soldiers—his wife, his son and daughter,
perhaps the ashes of a girl he loved in childhood.
Outside their window
a Sun Bird and Dead Sea Sparrow fly
from everlasting to everlasting.
Later he covers my head with his hands, blessing me,
later unable to walk alone he holds onto my hand
with so much strength he comforts me.

CHINESE PRAYER

God of Walls and Ditches, every man's friend,
although you may be banqueting in heaven
on the peaches of immortality
that ripen once every three thousand years,
protect a child I love in China
and on her visits to the United States,
if your powers reach this far, this locality.
You will know her because she is nine years old,
already a beauty and an artist. She needs more
than the natural protection of a tree on a hot day.
You have so many papers,
more than the God of Examinations,
more than the God of Salaries,
who is not for me, because I am self-employed.
It may help you find her to know her mother
was once my bookkeeper,
her brother is a God in the family,
who at six still does not wipe his bottom.
Protect her from feeling worthless.
She is the most silent of children.
She has given me so many drawings and masks,
today I offered her fifty dollars for a painting.
Without a smile she answered,
"How much do you get for a metaphor?"
Sir, here is a little something to keep the incense burning,
remember her to the Almighty God whose character is Jade.

THE STARTLING

When I saw the Greek hunter
painted on the fifth-century red-figured pot
was changed into a startled fawn
because he watched a goddess bathe naked,
and that his own dogs tore him to pieces,
I had already changed from myself
to another self, further apart
than man from fawn.
When coming out of my self, I woke you
in the middle of the night to carry you off
to the sea; I stopped three times
to ravish you; you took me beyond my life,
raced me from great distance to great distance,
till helpless I fell in your lap
and said I was near death.
You lifted the heavy beast's head,
still snorting and groaning, kissed me
and washed your blood from my face,
stroked me and called me "sweet one"—
then you sang your siren song,
told me how I would be remembered,
that sleep and death were brothers,
that the sirens defeated by poetry
were changed into the great boulders
on which the city of Naples,
so well known to lovers, was founded.
I kissed you and you asked gently,
since you were young and I was not,
what Dido asked Aeneas
who was soon to go to war:
"Will you leave me without a son
of your name?"

A RIFF FOR SIDNEY BECHET

That night in Florence,
forty-five years ago,
I heard him play
like "honey on a razor,"
he could get maple syrup
out of a white pine,
out of a sycamore,
out of an old copper beech.
I remember that summer
Michelangelo's marble
naked woman's breasts,
reclining Dawn's nipples—
exactly like the flesh I ached for.
How could Dawn behind her clouds hurt me?
The sunrise bitch was never mine.
He brought her down. In twelve bars of burnt sugar,
she was his if he wanted her.

SOME FLOWERS

For Irving Howe

In a world where you are asleep with your fathers,
in that part of the forest where trees read,
your tree still reads to us. Tonight your branches bend over
Conrad, Trotsky, Saba,
the evergreen Irish.

Joyce hated flowers,
his wife put a houseplant on his grave.
There are no socialist flowers
yet the balmiest wind favors
a more even distribution of wealth.
Some have seen among the flowers religious orders,
proved a rose a Christian,
while of course they pruned away the Jew.

It is easier for me to believe flowers
know something about wages and hours,
a fair day's pay for a fair day's work in the sun,
than to believe in the resurrection of the flesh.

When you died, the Amalgamated Clothing Workers
of America published a notice
of their mourning and sent flowers.
Your last sweet note that reached me after your death,
I left on the dashboard in a book,
the way they used to press dry flowers.
As I drove along in Canada,
it flew out of the window—
I thought it was a bill.

THE LAST JUDGMENT

Pushing up through a hole in the red marble floor of heaven
a black prisoner sentenced to death,
shows his tattooed resurrected flesh:
a blue tear under the outside corners of his eyes,
on his arm two copulating dragons,
their eyes a woman's breasts,
a pierced bleeding heart on his back the size of an eagle,
his chest bears the face of Christ.
Anathema, it cannot be true such unlikely flesh rises to heaven.

Now in the maw of heaven
I see poor losers shrouded with eternal ink—
it's a little like whistling against Bach's B-minor mass,
there is so much ecclesiastical counterfeit money around:
the anti-Christ silver dollar, the St. Sebastian dime.
Asleep on the marble floor a drowned sailor,
at his knee a cock, his wrists ringed with barbed wire;
a woman walks in circles,
her body still scented with the lilies of death,
her mouth the shape of her lovemaking,
a wolf's head on her shoulder,
its nose nestled between her breasts.
Beneath a huge egg hanging from a cord,
a woman who seems to be mad
says she will die if she sleeps alone,
a vine of tiny roses runs down both sides of her belly
to her bush still moist, a large bee put where the hair begins—
on her back, lovers beneath a tree in full foliage
and the motto: *God is the name of my desire.*
Anathema, it cannot be true such unlikely flesh rises to heaven.
Is it true Jewish children with tattooed numbers on their arms
keep their religion even in heaven?

111

I look at my own flesh with the dyes of age,
the craquelure of love and caprichos. How many nights
have I fallen asleep to the beat of the oars in a boat
with the adult passengers: summer, winter, autumn, spring—
not knowing who is the designer, who the boatman,
the needles writing all night like dreams,
awaking, as all of us, to an uncompleted world,
to the *Behold I am standing before Thy face.*

ROMANCE

I was not Eros with a limp, or sleepwalking,
even so on a December Sunday afternoon
sunning itself on a footbridge that was three planks
over a meandering dry stream,
I saw a small green snake that was perhaps a year
twist away at the first sight of me into the tall reeds
of the future, with time enough to found a nation.
I crossed the same planks, the heavy serpent
of old age oozed along behind me.
The sunlight on the bridge and the two snakes
were a sundial beyond the indications
of the world's Christian calendar.
Then I passed green fields of winter rye
already six inches high despite the early snow.
I whispered to myself:
Verde, que te quiero verde. Verde viento . . .
Follow the heart, follow the heart!

SATYR SONGS

"I want a hero: an uncommon want . . ."
BYRON, *Don Juan*

A common satyr and poet, I want a hero
who reaches up to the matter beneath
the stanza: eight lines, ten syllables or so,
as into underpants, who rhymes *faith*
and *death, hello* if he cares to with *Galileo,*
who recanted, but fathered before his death
Natural Philosophy and three natural daughters
baptized in the Arno's muddy waters.

I cheer for *love,* what some call *vice,*
what some call *sin,* some simply pleasure,
humping, romance, odd ways of making nice,
taking advantage of, taking the measure.
One wife's passion is another's sacrifice,
one man's poison is another's cure.
A little fornication rights all wrongs,
there are no commandments in the Song of Songs.

We are made of water, earth, air, and fire
in the image of the One you-know-Who,
whose hair in the wind is Hebrew barbed wire.
On the first day when the sun was brand new,
creation a blast, He simply took a flyer,
since in darkness there was little to do,
He made us—to drown us in the ocean
of the last full measure of devotion.

Not every lady returns from the dance
with the guy who brought her, anything written
by man or woman in honest ink may rinse
away in tears. Love's not an altered kitten

in the master's lap, fed on white mice.
For every French kiss there is a France,
for every bugger there is a Britain,
for every time I bite, twice I'm bitten.

I hate shoes, bare human feet on the floor.
Mozart loved to hear the sound of hooves
on oak, marble—sweet Köchel 44,
his concerto for woodwinds and satyr hooves,
brought satyrs to court before the Emperor.
Today you hear such music, such hooves
in Andalusian caves and orange groves,
in Greek cafés, and on the Mount of Olives.

When a boy, I first saw my lower half:
my goat hooves, my pecker, I shook in terror,
called it my sock apple tree for a laugh.
How many would eat my apples to the core,
would I father a kid, a faun, a calf,
as I stood helpless before the mirror,
the living proof of the Creator's error,
erotic errata, a kid who pees on the floor?

My mother told me Jesus was a satyr
so I wouldn't feel bad at Christmas without a tree,
that God was a lover, not a hater,
to button up my overcoat when the wind is free,
(she said she'd tell me about the Devil later),
to take good care of myself, she belonged to me.
She taught me to be silly, and to be good
which brightened the night sky of my childhood.

Further, she explained, "Be true to your phallus.
Live in the wilderness. The future is now, not eternity."
I loved the Aurora Borealis.
Hell was the city, heaven the country,

the woods, a field of wildflowers, my place.
One kiss in the country is worth ten in the city,
whatever the weather, I took days at random,
one at a time, in circles or in tandem.

Now, the question is, how can a good wife
live with a circumcised satyr from Queens
who thinks sin is cutting spaghetti with a knife,
childbirth the parable of spilled beans.
To understand this mystery, this hieroglyph,
each day she needs a Rosetta Stone, she preens
burrs, hay and lice from my graying plumage,
gently combs the old madness from my rage.

Centaurs teach, satyrs are autodidacts.
I have horns, not rays of light like Moses,
following the heart is my business, not facts,
or lines of reason. I chase the scent of roses,
waterfalls, meanings that fall through the cracks.
The day composes and decomposes—
love after love—I pay attention to rhyme,
to sunrise and sunset, not silly-billy time.

I have no time for clocks that tie up time's
two legs so the Gods only hop and jump—
sure to stumble on "is" or simple rhymes
for "was." My god makes the grasshopper jump,
frogs croak, the sun go down while the moon climbs
up to darkness. Love made the first atom jump.
I am entangled by love and untangled—
love the enchanting, love the newfangled.

When I heard the great god Pan was dead,
I asked did he die three deaths for us: goat,
man, and God, the hand of Saturn on his head?
He taught the ways of imperfection. Devout

Pan, you died so we might know Lust instead
of moderation, so we who cannot fly can float,
free as you taught us, our drunken hooves unsure,
walking the giddy clouds above our pasture.

The trick was not to know myself, I was not
human, so I could only pretend to be
a gentleman, a fish out of water, a What
is That?, a centaur, a mule, a donkey.
Let me be a well-written sentence, not
a blot on the human page, not poetry,
a satyr, a freak of nature, a growth,
a knot on a tree, a goat of my word, an oath.

I said, "I will never forget you, dear,"
but what is my never, never, never worth?
Once my "never" was worth fifty years;
you could take it to the bank, a piece of earth
you could mortgage. Now my life is in arrears,
it is late December, there is a dearth
of everything, years, months, days are hostile.
I will remember you, love, a little while.

My lady's touch has a way of whispering:
"It is summer, a perfect day—cloud
after cloud." . . . The world's a good for nothing
and a good for something. It is right that a hungry crowd
of seagulls attacks a fluke as if it were the world.
In the lucky world, still on the wing
love whispers, "It is summer, a perfect day."
May my lady's touch have its way.

2002, ALAS

Where are the birthday poems
for Stalin and Hitler,
the angelhair tarts for Franco?
Where are the sweets of yesteryear,
the party hats? Our revels are not over!
They are shooting rifles in the air
for bin Laden and Saddam.
Happy children
are making bombs of themselves
as never before.
Dreams of mass murder have only begun:
daydreams and wet dreams.
But where is the pastry?
Where are the poems?
Coming, coming, the children sing.
Coming, coming.

A SATYR'S COMPLAINT

It means little to me now when I am rusting away
that at dawn gods still roll out of our human beds,
that once I entered down the center aisle
at the Comédie Française, the Artemis of Ephesus
on my arm, all eyes on her rows of breasts and me.
"Who is the master of her ninety nipples?"
the public whispered. No one noticed I was in fact
a bronze satyr, my goat feet, my tail, my erect penis.
I loved confusion, chaos was paradise.
I found happiness, so to speak, on the ramps
and scaffolding of the Tower of Babel,
I danced holding a tambourine above my head
made from a brass Turkish sieve I called *time*.
Water, sacramental wine, ink once words, passed through.
In old Rome, I played the flute, but at the first sight
of my combed, perfumed, and throbbing lower half,
Lucretia thrust a dagger through her heart.
Later in Pisa, when on the Piazza a colossal
New Testament was carved in marble in Greek—
chapter and verse, I danced across Matthew, John,
Mark and Luke, leapt to Revelation, stars flashing
from my hooves. In the Basilica, virgins
lined up on their knees in white for first communion.
A proper satyr, I took half a dozen from behind.
The wafers danced on their tongues. Beautiful,
the little hearts of blood on white lace.
The Tower of Pisa leaned away from me in disgust.
I shouted back at the mob of tourists who attacked me:
You will never put out the fires of hell
with a nineteenth-century American candle-snuffer.
The devil is no one, a French-Canadian plaster loon.
Frightened by my mythological smell
a bronze horse reared up, broke away

from his handler. Mares turned their hindquarters
to the north wind, bred foals without the aid of stallions.
Born for blasphemy and lust, uncircumcised half-goat,
I made my way to the Holy Land.
I am proud my bronze prick was the clapper
in many a Jewish, Christian and Muslim belle.
I must have done something right,
Jew, Christian and Muslim chased after me
throwing stones: onyx, opals, diorite,
the glass eyes of their god.
I hid in the cold lawless night of Sinai,
my companions a snail, a skeleton of an eel.
Wise man, remember every giraffe farts above your head.
What have I stolen from myself, I thought.
How can I pay myself back in kind?
The sun and moon survive absolutely without conscience.

SEPTEMBER 11TH: A FABLE

You caterpillars, who want to eat
until there is not one familiar leaf on our living tree,
in New York there are bees that will bore into your belly,
sleep with your striped velvet over their eyes,
with their feet on your heart,
that, waking, will eat their way out of your soft belly.
I promise you would prefer
the quick sharp beak of a crow.
Become a butterfly.

A DENTIST

I dream I am Saddam Hussein's U.S. Army dentist.
I open his mouth, the color of a mop that has scrubbed blood
from a prison floor. His soul, the smell of his breath,
rises up in my face: vomit and eau de cologne.
It isn't every day I have a mass murderer in my chair.
I whistle for courage the staccato opening bars
of the overture to *The Marriage of Figaro*,
when my drill hits his nerve I hold every note.
He gives me a look of contempt that says
you are only a Jew dentist, not a torturer.
I put the removable bridge of his soul back
in his mouth and tell him to rinse.
Ashamed, I remember George Washington
had five slaves' teeth pulled out and fixed in his bridge.

RETURN TO ROME

Today in Rome, heading down
Michelangelo's *Spanish Steps*,
under an unchanging moon,
I held on to the balustrade,
grateful for his giving me a hand.
All for love, I stumbled over the past
as if it were my own feet. Here, in my twenties,
I was lost in love and poetry. Along the Tiber,
I made up Cubist Shakespearean games.
(In writing, even in those days,
I cannot say it was popular to have "subjects"
any more than painters used sitters. But I did.)
I played with an ignorant mirror for an audience:
my self, embroiled with personae
from *Antony and Cleopatra*. Delusions of grandeur!
They were for a time my foul-weather friends—
as once I played with soldiers
on the mountainous countryside of a purple blanket.

WEDDING INVITATION

I leap high as I can for joy, higher than you think I can.
My son writes he is marrying in September in Fiesole,
I leap over my dogs, whom he invited,
although they don't understand weddings.
You, dear reader, are also invited,
after all the funerals I brought you to.
I've often played a drum major in a brass band called hope—
even when the band wasn't there. I suggest to my son
he ready his foot to break the wineglass
in memory of the destruction of the Temple. If he doesn't care to,
I'll leave the wineglass around, so it may break
by happy accident. I never broke a wineglass
except when it fell off the table, or in rage. My best advice:
the usual public vows are not for nothing, when there's a problem
talk it over. I hope family history does not weigh heavier than love
and honorable intention. Bless you both,
now let the centaurs and Russian dancers in.

SONG OF IMPERFECTION

Whom can I tell? Who cares?
I see the shell of a snail protected by a flaw
in its design: white is time, blue-green is rot,
something emerging in the rough dust, the unused
part of a shape that is furious and calm.
In aging grasses, knotted with their being,
the snail draws near the east bank of the pond,
not because that is where the morning sun is,
but out of coastal preference, raising
a tawny knotted counterwhirl
like a lion cub against its mother's haunch,
anus of a star. But let the conch stand
in the warm mud, with its horn become an eye,
suffering the passion of any snail:
a hopeful birth, a death, an empty tomb.
I'd walk with this horned eye, lip-foot after lip-foot,
beyond the dry wall of my life, backward
into the sacramental mud, where the soul begins to reason—
as on that afternoon Aristotle dissecting
squid proclaimed "the eternity of the world."
There is not a thing on earth without a star
that beats upon it and tells it to grow.

POST-SURGERY SONG

My surgeon went harrowing like Christ in Hell,
dug a virtuous pagan tumor from my kidney.
"What do I look like inside?" I asked. "Just like every other,
except the distance from your kidney to your heart."
"Aah," I thought, "I have a certain lonely alley inside,
like the Vicolo della Bella Donna in Florence."
I thought I knew the catechism of the bladder,
the daily questions and answers, until blood clots
clogged my drain, once a Roman fountain.
My bladder swelled as if giving birth,
then for all the world—a razor blade in the anus.
I cried uncle. Christ and surgeon,
if you believe merely thinking it
is the same as driving in the nails,
leave my wound! Physician, heal Thyself.

A REFRESHMENT

In our new society, all the old religious orders and titles
are ice creams: Rabbis, Priests, Mullahs,
Gurus, Buddhists, Shiites, Sunni, Dominicans,
Franciscans, Capuchins, Carmelites—ice cream,
never before have the kids had such a choice of flavors,
never before have the Ten Commandments
been so cool in summer. I believe
when the holy family rested on their flight to Egypt,
in the desert heat, they had a little mystical lemon or orange ice,
before chocolate and vanilla crossed the unnamed Atlantic.
Let us pray, not for forgiveness, but for our just dessert.

HOT NEWS, STALE NEWS

Herodotus tells us in an election year
Pisistratus, the Athenian tyrant,
wanting the protection of a god,
got the biggest beautiful woman he could find,
dressed her in silver and gold armor,
proclaimed her the goddess Athena
and drove through the streets of Athens
with the goddess at his side.
In our elections, every candidate
wants to be photographed
going to or coming from Jesus.
One declared, "Jesus is in my heart,"
but when he refused to stay
the death warrants for a hundred or so,
his Jesus was silent.

Our presidential candidates,
like Roman emperors,
favor the death penalty,
but in two thousand years there is a difference.
No candidate would do it for fun, or think death
a competent sentence for cutting down trees
or killing deer, as in 18th century England.
It's not all blood and circus:
when Camus asked de Gaulle,
"What can a writer do for France?"
The President replied: "Write well!"
Have you heard what's new on the Rialto:
since Pope John Paul declared anti-Semitism a sin,
hell has been so crowded,
you can't find a decent room there at a hotel.

THE FILM CRITIC IMAGINAIRE

He found his good wife weeping alone
when their friend's infidelity was discovered.
She had long pretended her husband's playing around
was like filmmaking: a take here, a take there,
out of sequence, everything but their life together
would end up on the cutting room floor.
Now she wept at breakfast,
forgot to pick up his suit at the cleaners,
and wept over that.
Angered, he realized his friend's infidelity
had held a full-length mirror to his own,
that the friend's behavior was unacceptable:
he had inconvenienced the distinguished critic,
the reader, the Anglophile, the man of the left.
For some days, my life was a fly buzzing around his head—
he swatted with the *Times*.

THE WATCH

See, there are two snakes copulating.
Watch long enough, like Tiresias
you will become male and female,
no longer know your mother or father.
First in your mother's belly you had a snake's heart,
then chamber by chamber you grew a human heart.
Concealed at night, you do not see the body,
but the heat around the body—the subjunctive heat
after wish and desire. In the garden at night
you cannot tell snake from human.
The theater is dark, the play is a comedy:
someone before death is begging for ten last syllables.

THE FAMILY

After P.A. Cuadra

Maria, sister, the story is—
it was the end of days.
Everything collapsed and we were left
in the street with what we wore,
twelve brothers and sisters trembling
and Mama wanting to put her arms around each of us.
At that moment, we were suffocating in the dust, listening
to the death rattle of the world.
At that moment I was thinking, "Papa,"
you understand, you already know
the ways of our father,
"I'm going to look for him," I said,
my poor mother screaming,
the brothers and sisters weeping.
But what can you do when everything falls,
when time succumbs, what remains
except looking for your father?
How often we said to him, "Father,
charity begins at home."
He, you know, always in the clouds,
always giving to everyone,
but demanding of us.
I ran through those black streets
while the whole city rose up
in dust and lamentation.
The shadows threw stones at me.
I felt rage, the deaf rage of a son
against a father
who abandons him,
and I blamed him
as if he were the author of Tenebrae,
the fist of destruction.

It may be—I thought—he's helping others. And so it was.
Do you remember Juan,
the caretaker? Remember
Juan, the one who left him with all the work in the field
and ran off with a prostitute?
I came across our father with his hands bleeding
rescuing Juan,
I saw him carrying Juan.
He looked at me with his gentle eyes: "Help me!"
he said. I should have shouted,
"Father, Father,
why have you abandoned us?"
It's useless! You how he is,
he always
abandons the flock
for a lost sheep.

IT CAME DOWN TO THIS

To Arnold Cooper

A mile from the Atlantic,
in your living room with the books and flowers
and the painting of fields behind your house,
facing Mecox bay, home to some two hundred swans,
fifty of which I have known since they were born,
it came down to this: I saw the room a little tilted
and you saw it straight, and when you proved it with a ruler
and leveler I fought back. The ruler might be wrong,
I have no faith an inch is equal to any other inch.
There are no equal numbers,
there is just an agreement as to what they mean.
I pity the violinist who just plays the notes.
But the roof of your house is not a sonata,
or your apple tree a violin, whoever plucks the fruit.
And worse, you, old friend, know better than I
the uniqueness of human beings,
you measured hoping to prove me right. I remember
once when we had caught a stringer full of bass
I tied them to the oarlock with a double hitch
I learned in the navy. When we came ashore
my knot had slipped—the trophy fish gone.
Even that, you forgave me with an archaic smile.
We are the same age, equals before the law,
but one will slip away under the waterlilies
before the other. Whoever slips away first,
proving me right about the ceiling, the roof, and inches—
the other shall hold a kind of grudge.

THE BLACK MAPLE

After an August Atlantic hurricane,
no curled brine-drenched leaf
was at first to Katherine's eye
a Monarch butterfly,
yet she telephoned the news:
flights of deceived Monarchs
had dropped down on her Black Maple
till she could not tell
leaf from butterfly.
In the morning when I arrived
only the tree of metaphor was there,
the butterflies gone to Mexico,
Katherine and her lover, soon to marry,
returned to Manhattan
to practice medicine and music.
Left behind by so much storm and flutter,
I have almost lost count of the seasons.

DARK CLOUDS

From whose breast does the milk of madness course?
I or he, an 18-year-old boy makes up his address,
the deaths of his parents still alive, his father's suicide.
I or he woos a girl, feigning his coming blindness,
asked what he would farm—*rifles*, he smiles.
I or he memorized Milton.
I or he never learned to say a prayer out loud
so God would hear us. Speaking to ourselves
as if to the Lord, he and I are two persons,
three, four, five, a multitude
climbing out of the mouth of a Leviathan.
My mother's breast wept, losing its milk.
He and I became the nurslings of dark clouds.

HOW I GOT TED ROETHKE'S
RACCOON-SKIN COAT

I gave my friend a lovely naked woman
dancing with a tambourine above her head,
a red terracotta plaque by Renoir.
With a laugh he gave me ten dead raccoons,
a blue and gold lining: his raccoon-skin coat,
made for hard Michigan winters and football games,
with a pocket inside for a whiskey flask.
Later, I sent to Seattle my English homburg
that flew cheering for him across America.
He told me to keep his blue pajamas
he left behind, sent back love and this:
"Robert Traill Spence Lowell
lays on his effects with a trowel,
I put them with Ginsberg's *Howl*,
the works of Robert Traill Spence Lowell."

FOR VIRGINIA ON HER 90TH BIRTHDAY

We know at ninety sometimes it aches to sing
or to sit in any chair, that words, music, love, and poetry
sometimes trip over each other.
Virginia, teach me not to walk steadily into the grave,
but to trip over it, to do the funny dance of the good long life.
It's easy as one, two, three. But what is one,
what is two, and where is three?
A good death is like a black butterfly
born too soon during a mild winter.

JUNE 21ST

Just when I think I am about to be tilted
on a table for death to eat—my friend arrives
playing a harmonica. It is my birthday.
He sings a little song that is a poem
written for the occasion.
How does he know the day I was born
the midwife laughed, enthusiastic
over the size of my head, chest and penis?
My mother must have told him.

My years are sheep, I shepherd them night and day,
I live with their "ba-ba."
They much prefer his harmonica to a pan-pipe.
Some years graze near me, others wander
across the valley out of sight.
I have two dogs, one dog can't do the job.
My 57th year keeps mounting my early years,
my 63rd year is giving it hard to my 57th,
my dogs are running in circles, barking for joy.

PHAETON: AN OVIDIAN FOLLY

Canto One

News reached Helios the Sun God,
as sounds of war, prayers,
the distant traffic of the world sometimes does:
a handsome boy was nearing the sun in a chariot,
in danger of catching fire. The boy had passed through
India, asking anyone old enough to be wise:
"Can the Sun God be my father?"
School friends had made fun of the fatherless boy,
although his mother Clymene explained
she met Helios by chance in an orchard.
"I loved him because he made the flowers bloom.
March became summer in an hour. The Sun
bit into me and the orchard—as if we were one apple,
and you were born."

Phaeton's chariot arrived at the palace barely singed.
The God of Fire had turned his face away.
He met his son at the flaming doorway.
"Before you ask, Phaeton, what your mother said is true.
You are my son. To celebrate our meeting
I will stock the northern lakes with sunfish."
The God noticed the boy's hair was flaming red.
He had his father's sunrise.
Phaeton, badmouthed the God:
"Where were you when I needed you to teach me
everyday lessons? I think you are a father
for a day." The God erupted,
"Who are you to think sunny? Still, there's sunrise
in you; ask me a favor, I will grant it—
I swear on the River Styx."
Phaeton grinned. "What I ask is your chariot.
I want to drive the winged horses for a day—

the car with the gold pulpit and axle,
the chrysolite wheels and silver spokes.
Keep your word to the River Styx and me."

The Sun God's voice darkened, "Yes.
Since the dawn of time that I am, there has been a form
in the sky, an eagle the size of an oak on its shoulder.
From the creature's entrails, you hear screams
of every living creature being devoured by their fathers.
Out of a vent in its tail leaks a drek of fathers and sons.
That creature would be called 'the Master of Creation'
if Zeus did not spike it.
Passing that monster that begat itself,
without me the winged horses
will panic, snap the reins you hanker for
made of gold hair left on my pillow."
The Sun God knew his words were useless.
The Hours were leading out the four winged horses.
"Phaeton, be a bright dawn, the hope of the world.
Drive westward, pyramids on your left. No horse
or boy ever learned from whippings or floods.
Look, the moon, my poor sister, is pale as a dove—
do not cause a drought. Because of me
there is no God of Disappointment."
The Sun God was mumbling now, afraid of his son's fate.
The boy jumped into his father's chariot,
shouted, "I'll be back tonight."

Canto Two

Rising from the East like any other day
Phaeton opened the night clouds with his whip,
turning them to fire. The horses knew
they were carrying a light, mortal thing that had no history.
Noon. The horses high in the heavens,
half a sky off course, smelled mares below,
dragged the godless flaming chariot earthward,
let off fountains of urine in Phaeton's face.
Phaeton's knees shook. He had to urinate.
He wished he never knew who his father was.
He wished his father had broken his oath.
He wished he were a bastard again.
Where is East, where is West? Who is North, who is South?
Now the eagle the size of an oak was coming toward him.

A wheel broke off, rolled in flames through Africa.
Crete and Sicily were under water, the Arctic—mud.
China was a flaming paper lantern,
rivers promised swans in the coming summer boiled.
The world's olive groves, some sacred, were hissing embers.
Parnassus was blackened marble.
The Earth Goddess called to Zeus,
"Oh my great lover, all my harvests,
all the years of laboring, good farmers I blessed, gone,
the pain of the plough I bore, come to nothing.
Strike down the sun's vainglorious boy!"
Zeus smacked Phaeton out of the burning clouds.
Helios the helpless Sun God wept.
For the first time since chaos he took off his golden helmet.
He felt like a coal-miner in a pit. In darkness he shouted,
"Zeus, you bugger, you seducer of mortal wives
and boys, disguise yourself as the great prick you are
and piss out the fires. Zeus, may you be deposed by Jews,
Christians, Muslims, Hindus, Baptists and Buddhists.

I owe nothing to the world. I see the living live by stealing fire.
Since I was the Dawn of Time, I labored.
How often I found my bright work dull.
Don't you think I wanted to command the Sea,
make War, or Music?"

Zeus mumbled, "My thunderbolt is not a question mark."
Every God and Goddess yawned. The Sun's flaming tears fell
into what rivers were left on Earth, making amber
that would one day become gifts between lovers,
recalled in the Canticle of Canticles, the Song of Songs.

Canto Three

After years of darkness, Helios took pity on the Earth Goddess,
with Eros on his shoulder, he turned his face toward Earth.
There was sunlight, good tempests and good blizzards.
The Earth bloomed. There were crops and farm houses,
oil lamps, fires under soupkettles, marble cities, slums again.
An old Greek, not an oracle, only a clever fellow
said: "These days, you almost never see a naked swimmer—
the Earth is filling with burning dumps and battlefields—
an insult to the Earth Goddess."
Someone shouted across the port of Athens,
"You will never crucify Apollo!" The Greek wrote in a letter:
"The Sun can never be made to look ridiculous.
You cannot get a hook into a Leviathan,
catch him with a line, or carry him to market.
You cannot get a word out of him, or have a covenant with him.
Sooner battle the Leviathan than the Sun."
The Sun had long since called back his winged horses,
whipped them and drowned them in flames.
Now every day is like every other to the Sun.

PROPHECY

An oracle told me
an elephant in a zoo
will pick up a child
in a red shirt, higher
than he has ever been
in a swing or a seesaw—
the trunk an S
over the elephant's head.
His father will drop
his ice cream cone,
the kid will wave to the world
hello, goodbye—
then swoosh across the moat.
That's the way it will happen.
You will call the mother
saying, "Darling,
I have something to tell you . . ."
the taste of chocolate
still in your mouth.
And you are the father
and you are the child.

STOWAWAY

1

Aging, I am a stowaway in the hold of my being.
Even memory is a finger to my lips.
Once I entered down the center aisle
at the Comédie Française, the Artemis of Ephesus
on my arm, all eyes on her rows of breasts and me.
"Who is this master of her ninety nipples?"
the public whispered.
Now the ocean is my audience,
I see in secret my last secret.

2

Mid-December, my old felt hat that I could have imagined
myself leaving behind in a restaurant for eternity
blew out into the Atlantic. The damn thing so familiar
I saw myself wearing it even into the deep,
an aging Narcissus, in white foam and northern sunlight,
on my way to becoming a conch. It is like seeing music
this growing from flesh and bone into seashell:
undulating salts become a purple mantle,
and the almost translucent
bivalve of memory and forgetting closes.

3
Asleep in the Garden
&
The Intelligence of Clouds

HANNIBAL CROSSING THE ALPS

He urged his starving elephants upward into the snows,
the barges still smelling of Mediterranean brine,
packed with huddled troops, men of Carthage
in ice-covered armor, some wearing desert sandals
wrapped in leaves, elephants up to their necks in snow,
trumpeting, their trunks grabbing at crumbling clouds of snow.
The colossal gray boulders swayed, moved upward,
some tumbled back into the echoing ravines.
An avalanche, forests of ice fell on Africa.
In the morning soldiers gathered remnants of red and blue silk,
dry sardines and beans, gold goblets still sandy
from desert victories, live turtles meant for soup,
a tangle of chained goats and sheep meant for sacrifice.

O you runners, walkers, horsemen, riders of bicycles,
men of sense and small gesture, commuters like me,
remember Hannibal came down from the Alps
into the warm belly of Italy, and conquered.
It was twenty years later in another place,
after errors of administration and alliance,
that he poisoned himself. What is remembered?
His colossal head asleep on the sand of Tunis,
a few dates, confusion between victories and defeats,
his elephants.

ANNUNCIATION

I saw a virgin who did not want to be
impregnated by words—but I do,
or did I see her pushing off the unwanted angel
when it was over, her humped-back cat hissing,
sensing perhaps the human, inhuman, natural son.
The loudest sound I ever heard came from within my ear:
babble and chaos, twins inside me, as if word and verb
from the beginning were without pause, stop, cesura—
all words meaningless, life without time and weather.
Did I hear my death conceived inside my ear,
like a child some call "the Savior"?

THE POET

He stared at a word and saw his face,
in every noun and every verb—his own face.
He could understand if he saw his face
in words like ocean, or on a blank page
or in anything that might mirror him,
but he saw his own face in *buts* and *ands*,
in *neither nor*, in *which* and *whose* and *what*.
In the names of others living and dead
he saw his own face.
The moment his senses came into play,
at the very edge of any perception, in light or darkness,
the word became his flesh
with his obscene mouth, his poisonous eyes.
Secretly he drew close to certain words
he hoped might not be his face, words he misspelled
in languages he barely knew, but every letter
was hair and tooth. What was not his face
was wordlessness—wordless tears, wordless laughter—
that never came to vowel or consonant.

LETTER TO THE BUTTERFLIES

1

Dear Monarchs, fellow Americans,
friends have seen you and that's proof,
I've heard the news:
since summer you traveled 5,000 miles
from our potato fields to the Yucatan.
Some butterflies can bear what the lizard would never endure.
Few of us can flutter away from the design:
I've seen butterflies weather a storm
in the shell of a snail, and come out of nowhere
twenty stories up in Manhattan.
I've seen them struggling on the ground.
I and others may die anonymously,
when all exceptionalism is over,
but not like snowflakes falling.
This week in Long Island
before the first snowfall, there is nothing left
but flies, bees, aphids, the usual.

2

In Mexico
I saw the Monarchs of North America gather,
a valley of butterflies surrounded
by living mountains of butterflies—
the last day for many.
I saw a river of butterflies flooding
through the valley, on a bright day black clouds
of butterflies thundering overhead,
yet every one remained a fragile thing.
A winged colossus wearing billowing silk
over a sensual woman's body
waded across the valley,

wagons and armies rested at her feet.
A village lit fires,
and the valley was a single black butterfly.

3

Butterflies,
what are you to me
that I should worry about your silks and powders,
your damnation or apotheosis,
insecticides and long-tongued lizards.
Some women I loved are no longer human.
I have a quarrel with myself for leaving my purpose,
for the likes of you, beauties I could name.
Sooner or later
I hope you alight on my gray stone
above my name and dates, questioning
my bewilderment.
Where is your Chinese God of walls and ditches?
Wrapped in black silk I did not spin,
do I hold a butterfly within?
What is this nothingness they have done to me?

FOR MARGARET

My mother near her death
is white as a downy feather.
I used to think her death was as distant
as a tropical bird, a giant macaw, whatever that is—
a thing I have as little to do with
as the distant poor.
I find a single feather of her suffering,
I blow it gently as she blew
into my neck and ear.

A single downy feather is on the scales,
opposed by things of weight, not spirit.
I remember the smell of burning feathers.
I wish we could sit upon the grass
and talk about grandchildren
and great-grandchildren.
A worm directs us into the ground.
We look alike.

I sing a lullaby to her about her children
who are safe and their children.
I place a Venetian lace tablecloth
of the whitest linen on the grass.
The wind comes with its song
about things given that are taken away
and given again in another form.

Why are the poor cawing, hooting,
screaming in the woods?
I wish death were a whippoorwill,
the first bird I could name.
Why is everything so heavy?
I did not think

she was still helping me to carry
the weight of my life.
Now the world's poor are before me.
How can I lift them one by one in my arms?

THE SWIMMER

I remember her first as a swimmer:
I saw my mother swimming, her arms reaching out
across giant ocean waves,
swimming through the breakers of the Atlantic.
I stood on the shore,
knowing almost nothing, unable to go to her—
dumbfounded by the wonder of it.
It was long before I could dress myself,
I was a little older than the weeping Chinese child
sitting alone in the rubble of the Nanking bombing—
barely old enough to be read to,
not able to tell time or count.
When I had that kind of knowledge, in her old age
she showed me herself naked, the tubes and the sack.
An hour later she said, "I must have been crazy."
Then she swam off again and never came back.
For a few days I awoke as that child again.
Now I have learned a kind of independence.
It is mostly in dreams she comes back, younger or older,
sometimes fresh from the joy of the swim.

LETTER TO AN UNKNOWN

Five centimeters, already Chinese,
in your mother's womb, pre–intellectual,
about sixty days. Sounds can see you,
music can see you. Fu Xu your father,
I introduce you to him, he is a painter
already saving for your education, preparing
to carry you on his shoulders to museums.
Zhu Ming your mother holds you close
as it is possible to hold a being close,
rare as an Empress, Freudian Chinese therapist,
she will teach you the joys and sorrows
of writing Chinese. May you spend
many happy years washing ink from your hands.
You have made the Great Wall of China bleed.
Who am I? Something like a tree
outside your window: after you are born,
shade in summer, in winter my branches
heavy with snow will almost touch the ground,
may shelter deer, bear, and you.

ALEXANDER FU

Surrounded by a great Chinese wall of love,
he is already three weeks old and has a name.
His mother combs his hair with her hand, nurses him.
Soon he will learn the tragic news: the world is not all love.
He has already begun to earn a living,
a little of his poopoo was just put in a flower pot.
The least part of him bears the seal of his Manufacturer.

ALEXANDER'S FIRST BATTLE

Now that you are looking over the edge of the world,
who will blame you for refusing to exchange
your mother's warm breast for rubber and warm glass?
Will you ever again be content? There will be laughter
and music, the solace of small talk, the solace
of art or science, twelve-year-old whiskey.
You will search the earth through hard years
to find somewhere in a timeless bed, or Venice,
or God forbid in the back seat of a car,
the return of such contentment. Alexander,
fight the bottle, fight it with all your being.
I will fight at your side.

ALEXANDER FU TO STANLEY

Big fool, my ancestors understood
we live in two societies: time and that other society
with its classes and orders, which you, Mr. America,
like to think you can ascend or descend at will.
Do I, a baby,
have to tell you there are laws that are not legislated,
judges neither appointed nor elected?
You are wetting your pants to talk to me.
Did it ever cross your mind I like to be ten months old,
going on eleven? You are trying to rob me of my infancy
because I have all the time in the world, and you don't.
On this May evening passing round the world
I probably have more diapers on the shelf
than you have years to go. I wish every time I shit
you'd have another year. Now that's an honest wish,
better than blowing out candles.
(Secretly you want to learn from me.)
You say I look like a prophet. Did it ever cross your mind
I would just like to be a bore like you?
Stop thinking about the Jew, Christian, Buddhist, Taoist thing!
The Long March wasn't from Kovno to Queens.
In summa: you are old and I am young,
that's the way it should be. I have better things to think about
than are dreamt of in your post-toilet-trained world.

LETTER TO ALEXANDER FU

A few days after your first birthday,
we had lunch on soup I made for grown-ups,
your father took you from your mother's arms,
carried you around our house to show you the sights;
he passed a painting of barren Sarah offering Hagar
to Abraham, old as I am. Then he stopped
before a half-naked lady looking in a mirror,
her two faces made you laugh.
In the library he showed you a family
resting on a hillside while their donkey grazed.
He did not tell you who they were, or that they were
on their way to Egypt.
He explained in Chinese and English:
"In this kind of painting, you must show the source of light.
The sunlight is behind the olive tree, the donkey
and sleeping father are in shade."
He named the colors, showed you a rainbow over a river.
You clapped hands and danced in his arms,
screeched so loud for joy, the dogs barked.
Next he came to an archangel with black wings
leading a boy carrying a fish.
He didn't tell you the boy will take fish gall,
put it into his father's eyes and cure his blindness.
Your father is a Chinese artist with a green card,
you are an American citizen in his arms.

Five years have passed. I read this letter to Alexander,
asked him what it meant.
He said, "It means Daddy likes me.
He should have explained in English before Chinese.
Abraham lived a hundred years,
had a baby and made God laugh.
God tells the heart what to do,
the heart tells the brain what to do.
I like that story, I want to take it home."

TO ANGELINA, ALEXANDER'S COUSIN, WHOSE CHINESE NAME MEANS HAPPINESS

She lies naked, five days old,
a chance that history might be kindness and love,
a chance the size and strength of her hands—
the rarest Chinese-American beauty,
certain to break hearts.
May she teach her children Mandarin,
Tu Fu and calligraphy,
however busy the city.

May she know the joy of singing,
may she play a musical instrument,
may she find her own way in the wilderness.
Under the seven halts in the sky,
may she and her brother who is four
having sucked from the breast
of one mother, swear on her dark nipple
to be true to her nature.

I remember an ancient Chinese poet
saw a nine-year old beauty
in a rose garden.
No one near the child
would speak except in whispers—
such was the power and burden of beauty.

After ten ancient years
the poet returned to marry her.
Later, the French and British
in Beijing ravished the sacred garden,
pillaged the Summer Palace.
It was not enough for the Brits
to have roses bloom at Westminster in December . . .

Angelina, you are five days old
and I have some 28,000 days.
If I were not married, I would wait.

DOG

Until the rain takes over my life I'll never change,
although I know by heart the Lord's Prayer
and the prayer Christ prayed to his father
in John, chapter 17, sanctifying himself.
Trying to convert me would be like teaching a dog to drive a car
just because it likes to go out for a drive—and save the poor mutt
from the greater or lesser vehicles of Buddhism.
On the other hand I am a dog that has been well treated
by his master. He kisses me and I lick his face. When he can
he lets me off the leash in the woods or at the beach.
I often sleep in his bed.

CHINA SONNET

On a red banner across the center of this poem
there is painted in gold Chinese letters:
"Strive to Build Socialist Spiritual Civilization."
On the right side hangs a red banner saying,
"Intellectuals: Cleaning Shithouses for Ten Years
in the Cultural Revolution Clears the Head."
Down the left side is pasted
a lantern-thin red and black paper-saying,
"When Spring Comes Back, the Earth is Green."
Off the page is China: the people give little importance
to what they call "spring couplets," the paper-sayings
pasted with wheat-flour and water above the lintels
and down the sills of peasant houses. They seldom notice
they enter and depart through the doors of poetry.

APRIL, BEIJING

Some of the self-containment of my old face
has been sandblasted away. The "yellow wind"
is blowing and my mouth and face burn
from the Gobi dust that scorches the city
after its historic passage over the Great Wall.
When I was young, I hosed the Atlantic salt
off my body—the salt was young too.

In China, "ashes to ashes and dust to dust"
means something more; work, no matter how cruel,
is part prophecy. Workers in fields
that were Chinese eight thousand years ago,
their plows and terraces a kind of calligraphy,
face the living and the dead, whose windy fortress
takes on a mortal form: the Great Wall.
Even here the North Wind abducts a beauty.
Never before have I heard ancient laughter.
In China, I can taste the dust on my own grave
like salt. The winter coal dust shadows every wall
and window, darkens the lattice and the rose,
offers its gray society to the blue cornflower,
the saffron crocus, the red poppy.

                  The moon
brushed by calligraphy, poetry and clouds,
touched, lowered toward mortality—
to silk, to chess, to science, to paper,
requires that the word and painting respond
more intimately to each other, when the heart
is loneliest and in need of a mother,
when the ocean is drifting away,
when the mountains seem further off.

The birds sing in the dark before sunrise
because sunlight is delayed by dust and the sound
of a poet grinding his own ink from stone
according to the moon's teaching.
I am happy to be here, even if I can't breathe.
The emperor of time falls from a tree,
the dust rises.

ON TRYING TO REMEMBER TWO CHINESE POEMS

I've forgotten the book, the poet,
the beauty of calligraphy,
the poems made to be seen and read out loud,
two lost songs on hanging scrolls
stolen by foreigners . . .

White as frost,
a piece of freshly woven silk
made a fan, a bright moon.
She, or my lady, kept a fan nearby,
its motion a gentle summer breeze . . .
he dreaded the coming of autumn
when the north wind breaks the summer heat
and the fan is dropped unwanted
into a lacquer box,
its short term of favor ended.

A catalog of beds:
riverbed, flower bed, family bed.
My mother died when I was three,
dreadful to be a child in baby clothes.
I climbed into her bed and tried to nurse,
clutching her body with all my strength;
not knowing she was dead I spoke to her,
called to her. I remember thinking,
before, when I wept and ached for her,
although she was sick she came to me,
she whispered and caressed me,
then the lamp went out
and my mother coughed by the chilly window.

. . . A night of restless birds.
Without warning
a great forest fire, a devouring flaming wind,
rolling mountains of fire
with nothing to stop them but the sea.
Woman is half the sky.

POSTCARD TO WALT WHITMAN FROM SIENA

Today I walked along the vaulted hall
of a Renaissance hospital opposite the Duomo
and I thought of you, Walt Whitman, in your forties,
writing letters for the wounded and dying.
This October Italian morning is clean as the air of Montauk.
In the sunlit galleries among medieval painters
there is a kind of gossip about the life of Christ
—the artists did not sign their names,
worked for the honor of illumination,
gold leaf, not leaves of grass.
I remember you sang Italian arias
and "The Star-Spangled Banner" in your bathtub.
To wash the horribly wounded,
you did not need to think of them as Jesus, but as themselves.
Walt, I saw a cradle shaped like a church you could rock.
Yesterday at five o'clock I heard the rosary
up to the "joys and sorrows" of the Virgin, had coffee,
then returned for the litany, metaphors about the Virgin:
star of the sea, lily of the valley, tower of ivory—
like you and your America.
Walt, I know you and the Virgin Mother
have conversation with the poor.
I try to listen.

FARCEUR

The first days of March,
the smell of the newborn in the air
brought his brays and imitations,
the miracles and illusions of everyday life:
birth and death as donkeys
chewing the same grasses, breaking the same wind.
Not myth, not document or hymn,
but a way of laughing by writing
and re-writing; as it turned out he wrote
a farce about the distance between fathers
and sons, mothers and daughters,
who reflect one another,
meet like water and sky
that only seem to touch at a distance.
In a garden under grape leaves,
he rested his head on books and wrote a letter
about the seasons passing more quickly,
the worship and praise his God had disregarded.
On the inner surface of a bowl, he wrote scripture,
poured water in, stirred until the writing was dissolved,
then filled his mouth, gargled, swallowed, and grinned.

LULLABY

I hear a Te Deum of "...Who are you to think...
touch religion like a hot stove,
hide bad news and the dead...a fool will light candles,
a fool will bless the children, a fool is ceremonious."
I see my first roadside wildflowers,
the lake—every sunfish nibble is a kiss.
On a summer afternoon
the clouds and I are useless brothers;
Eros carves his bow with a kitchen knife.

I read by the light of fire blazing in their hands:
my father who I thought would die forever,
my mother who I thought would live forever.
I won't forget the child who could not speak his name,
Rossini arias, the condoms on the floor,
the studying, the sweet and sour of moral purpose,
under a frowning etching of Beethoven.
The cuckoo clock was moved from room to room.
Age ten, I flew a red flag for revolution
in my bedroom and yearned for a better world.

I've made my family into an entertainment.
Once I named their symbols: the sewing basket,
fruits and animals, as their attributes.
I could show us as we were at home,
walking across a New York street or at the ocean
each brooding alone in the sand.
There is a lullaby children sing to the old.
The truth is, now in death we hold hands.

CENTAUR SONG

A creature half horse, half human,
my father herded his mares and women together
for song, smell and conversation. He taught me
to love wine, music and English poetry.
Like the Greeks he left the temple's interior
for priests, he observed outside
where he could see the pediment and caryatids.
If he saw a beauty out walking, or on a journey,
the proper centaur offered to carry her
over ice, or across a river—he'd bolt
to the edge of a wood, a place of sunlight.
He slid her gently down his back,
held her to him with a hoof.
Hooves cut. How could he touch with tenderness?
I feel his loneliness when I am just with horses,
or just with humans. There was a time
when he was tied to a tree,
so he could not go to one or the other.
Now his city crushed deep in the ground
has disappeared in darkness
—which is a theme for music.
He licked the blood from a trembling foal,
he galloped back to his books.
Today the North Wind fathers,
which is why it is said mares
often turn their hindquarters to the wind
and breed foals without the aid of stallions.

UNCERTAIN WEATHER

Uncertain weather.
The most aloof birds
come closer to the earth,
confused by the apparent
lowering of the clouds and sky.
I walk in these descending clouds.
Gulls set off.
The fish don't care.
I surf-cast a silver spoon
into the clouds
in the direction of the sea.

Last summer in Long Island
I saw a pair of white egrets
standing at the shoreline.
Now in Jamaica
I see hundreds swooping above me,
beyond Fern Gully
where the roads lead into fields of sugarcane,
the old slave plantations.

The flights of egrets remind me
of alarmed swallows—
then I see what they are doing:
hundreds of white birds
are trying to drive
a single buzzard out of the valley,
diving again and again to protect their nests.
In just a few days
I have become accustomed
to seeing egrets perched on cattle
or standing beside, motionless.

Now I see them fighting for life,
summoning whatever violence they have,
unable to be graceless.
One by one, not as a flock,
the birds dive, pursue,
do not touch.
Off the Caribbean,
a fresh afternoon wind
lifts the egrets higher
and gives the red-throated scavenger,
who must also feed its young,
a momentary passage
down into the tall moist grass.

LULLABY FOR TWINS

Sleep now little son, little daughter,
so young you have not yet smiled,
your penis and vagina have not yet
been filled with laughter.
You are helpless and wild.
It will come, the look of a smile,
the smile, the laughter,
the playing in bed and water,
your first devotion.
Sleep now on your mother's breast.
It will come a little after—
the sadness under the coverlet,
the plunge into the ocean,
the laughter.

IN FRONT OF A POSTER OF GARIBALDI

I

When my Italian son
admired a poster of Garibaldi
in the piazzetta of Venice,
a national father in a red shirt,
gold chain, Moroccan fez and fancy beard,
I wished the boy knew the Lincoln
who read after a day's work,
the commoner, his honesty.
My knees hurt from my life and playing soccer—
not that I see Lincoln splashing with his kids
in the Potomac. Lord knows where his dead son led him.

2

My son tells me Fortuna could have put
Lincoln and Garibaldi in Venice—
Garibaldi in red silk, Lincoln
in a stovepipe hat black as a gondola.
My son mimics Garibaldi:
"Lincoln, you may be the only man in the piazza
to log down the Mississippi
and walk back the 1,500 miles to Illinois
but you are still a man who calls all pasta macaroni.
How do you know where you are going?
Your shoes are straights, no lasts,
no right or left, no fashion, white socks.
How can the President of the United States
make such a *brutta figura*?"

3

I can't speak for Lincoln,
any more than I can sing for Caruso
—toward the end when Caruso sang,
his mouth filled with blood.
Not every poet bites into his own jugular:
some hunger, some observe the intelligence of clouds.
I was surprised to see a heart come out
of the torn throat of a snake. I know a poet
whose father blew his brains out
before his son was born, who still leads his son
into the unknown, the unknowable.

4

My son tells me I must not forget
Garibaldi fought for liberty in six countries
including Uruguay, he refused the command
of a corps that Lincoln offered, asked
to be head of the Union armies and for
an immediate declaration against slavery,
he was the "King's flag," defeated
the papal armies in 1866,
which gave the Jews equality in Italy.

5

I've always had a preference
for politics you could sing
on the stage of the Scala.
I give my son Lincoln and Garibaldi
as guardian angels.
May he join a party and a temple
that offer a chair to the starving and unrespectable.

We come from stock that on the day of atonement
asks forgiveness for theft, murder, lies, betrayal,
for all the sins and crimes of the congregation.
May he take his girls and bride to Venice,
may the blessings come like pigeons.
Lincoln waves from his gondola and whispers,
"I don't know what the soul is,
but whatever it is, I know it can humble itself."

CLOCKS

I

I pass a half-naked child
asleep on a marble slab in Grand Central Station.
I remember a painting: the Infant Christ
asleep on a red marble slab,
and another: the man, Christ Dead,
on the same red marble stone of unction.
The great iron clocks
in the railroad stations of Christendom
witness nothing,
they are simply above with their everydayness,
in natural, artificial and supernatural light.
I turn my head away from the faceless
puddles of drying urine
in the marble passageways
between nowhere and the street above.
I turn away from time's terrible sufficiency
that is, like God, in need of nothing whatsoever.
I do not know how to speak
for the poor of the world so hungry
God only appears to them as bread.

2

Last June under the horologe of the Italian sky,
my mind full of timetables and illusions,
I went back to Siena after forty years,
faithful to something, the city scolded
by San Bernardino of the flaming heart
for loving the Madonna so much it had forgotten Jesus.
I saw a painting of the kneeling Archangel

announcing to Mary a child will be born to her:
she wears two delicate, looped earrings,
from which hang two little gold crosses,
signs of the Crucifixion that has not yet occurred.

Time is nothing—an echo;
night and day are only a foreshadowing.
I have not yet disappeared.

ALLEGORY OF SMELL

His smile says he has had the smell of it,
flying the bitter end of a rooster tail
above his hat. In a torn army jacket
an old soldier pounds the tavern table.
They bring him an onion, garlic and a rose.
He discards the rose. He says, "To hell and back
a man stinks of what he is." He shouts:
"I myself am a sack of piss—thanks to brandy
mine smells like an apple orchard."
He remembers the gardens of women:
summer women, when they pass, enter
a man's soul through the nostrils, the consolation
the good Lord provides old soldiers.
A smell can be as naked as a breast.
His red eyes shine with tears from the onion he eats.

ALLEGORY OF EVIL IN ITALY

The Visconti put you on their flag: a snake
devouring a child, or are you throwing up a man
feet first? Some snakes hunt frogs, some freedom of will.
There's good in you: a man can count years on your skin.
Generously, you mother and father a stolen boy,
to the chosen you offer your cake of figs.
A goiter on my neck, you lick my ear with lies,
yet I must listen, smile and kiss your cheek
or you may swallow the child completely. In Milan
there is a triptych, the throned Virgin in glory,
placed on the marble below, a dead naked man
and a giant dead frog of human scale on its back.
There's hope! My eyes look into the top of my head
at the wreath of snakes that sometimes crowns me.

LOST DAUGHTER

I have protected the flame of a match
I lit and then discarded
more than I cared for you.
I had little to go on:
a postcard that came for no reason,
forty years ago,
that told me of your birth and name,
but not who was your father.
I would never give
my child your name.
In the woods and ditches of my life you
are less than a wildflower.
If you have a garden I
am less than melted snow.
I never held your hand
and this is the only bedtime story
I will ever tell you.
No love, no prayer, no flame.

SHOES

Home, I bang the sand out of my shoes.
I haven't the craft to make a goat's-belly bagpipe
from a shoe or the art to play it,
but I can see my cold wet shoes
as unwept-for bodies without a poet.
I speak for the leather ghosts of children.
I hold one up: a newborn infant without breath.
I cannot smack it into life. I face
mountains of shoes, endless lines of children
holding their parents' hands. I hold a shoe to my ear
like a seashell—hear a child's voice: "God is the old woman
who lived in a shoe, she had so many children . . ."
I hear the cries of cattle
begging for mercy in a slaughterhouse,
I smell the stink of the tannery.
I am a shoemaker, not a poet.

SONG FOR STANLEY KUNITZ

Creature to creature,
two years before we met
I remember I passed his table
at the Cedar Tavern.
He who never knew his father
seemed to view all strangers
as his father's good ghost,
any passing horse as capable
of being Pegasus, or pissing
in the street.
I who knew my father
was wary of any tame raccoon
with claws and real teeth.

At our first meeting forty years ago,
before the age of discovery,
I argued through the night
against the tragic sense of life;
I must have thought God wrote in spit.

I keep a petrified clam, his gift, on my desk.
These gray rings and layers of stone,
shape of a whale's eye, are old as any desert.
Measured against it, the morning, the Hudson River
outside my window are modern and brash,
the star of David, the cross, the hand of Fatima,
are man-made weather vanes.
My clamstone has weight and lightness.
It is my sweet reminder that flesh,
perhaps love, can remain in the natural world
long as poetry, tides, phases of the moon.
Tomorrow I shall wear it in my right eye,
a monocle for my talk on the relationship

between paleontology and anthropology.
Bless Celia, the cat of his middle years,
with her ribbons and hats, her pagan smile.
Bless the bobcat that was his in boyhood,
that killed a police dog in battle
on Main Street, Worcester, lost a foot for it
and had to be shot. A child with a leaf in his head,
he walked through devilsbit scabious,
marsh ragwort, vernal grass
until the meadows wept. Bless his first garden,
his bird feeder still there after eighty-one years.
Did any of his long-forgotten kindnesses
alter history a little?

What a *Luftmensch* he might have been,
his feet barely touching Commercial Street,
dancing home at three in the morning
with an ocean of money!
But how could he face the moon or the land
beside his house without a garden? Unthinkable.
I think what is written
in roses, iris and trumpet vine
is read by the Lord God.
Such a place of wild and ordered beauty
is like a heart that takes on the sorrows
of the world . . . He translates into all tongues.

LOWELL

He needed to be held, so his country
held him in jail awhile, nonviolent,
manic New Englander. In conversation
his hands moved across sentences, a music
of almost indiscernible Latin consonants
and Tennessee cakewalking vowels.
What was sight but a God to fool the eye?
Although he looked at you he stared away,
his eyes moved across some distant lawn
like the eyes on a peacock's tail.
Now his life of love, books and nightmares
seems 19th-century American allegory,
without the lofty language.
Could he imagine the lives of those who read
without the slightest attention to form,
the lives of readers of newspapers, books
of passing interest, or nothing at all—
their deaths a slip of the tongue?
A generation that might kill itself
gathered in him as if he were a public place:
to pray, agitate and riot. The man and flame he was
waved back and forth in the wind,
became all tongue. Falling off his ladder
in Ireland his last morning, "Whack. Huroo.
Take your partners," caught without time
to tell what happened, locked in a museum,
he tried to break through the glass door.
That evening in Manhattan he fell silent
on the floor of a taxi, the meter running.
Gluck said of early opera, "It stinks of music."
Cal, your life stank of poetry . . . "Buzz, buzz," he said,
a few bring real honey to the hive."

KRILL*

The red fisherman
stands in the waters of the Sound,
then whirls toward an outer reef.
The krill and kelp spread out,
it is the sea anemone that displays the of,
the into, the within.
He throws the net about himself
as the sea breaks over him.
The krill in the net and out of it
follow him. He is almost awash
in silver and gold.
How much time has passed.
He believes the undulation of krill
leads to a world of less grief,
that the dorsal of your smelt,
your sardine, your whitebait, humped
against the ocean's spine, cheers it
in its purpose.
The krill break loose, plunge down
like a great city of lights. He is left
with the sea that he hears
with its *if* and *then*, *if* and *then*, *if* and *then*.

---

* *a small crustacean, basic food of the whale*

187

THE BATTLE

When Yahweh spoke to me, when I saw His name
spelled out in blood, the pounding in my heart
separated blood from ink and ink from blood,
and Yahweh said to me, "Know your soul's name
is blood and ink is the name of your spirit.
Your father and mother longed with all their hearts
to hear my Name and title given to every generation."
When I heard the clear difference between my spirit
and my soul, I was filled with great joy,
then I knew my soul took the hillside
under its own colors, in the mirror red as blood,
and that my spirit stood its ground in the mirror
that is black as ink, and that there raged
a ferocious war in my heart between blood and ink.
The blood was of the air and the ink of the earth
and the ink defeated the blood, and the Sabbath
overcame all the days of the week.

YOU AND I

You are Jehovah, and I am a wanderer.
Who should have mercy on a wanderer
if not Jehovah? You create and I decay.
Who should have mercy on the decayed
if not the creator? You are the Judge
and I the guilty. Who should have mercy
on the guilty if not the Judge? You are All
and I am a particle. Who should have mercy
on a particle if not the All?
You are the Living One and I am dead.
Who should have mercy on the dead if not
the Living One? You are the Painter and Potter
and I am clay. Who should have mercy on clay
if not the Painter and Potter? You are the Fire
and I am straw. Who should have mercy on straw
if not the Fire? You are the Listener
and I am the reader. Who should have mercy
on the reader if not the Listener? You
are the Beginning and I am what follows.
Who should have mercy on what follows
if not the Beginning? You are the End and I am
what follows. Who should have mercy
on what follows if not the End?

SONG OF INTRODUCTION

Ancient of Days,
I hear the sound and silence, the *lumière*
of molds, disease and insects, I believe poetry
like kindness changes the world, a little.
It reaches the ear of lion and lamb, it enters
the nest of birds, the course of fish, it is water
in the cupped hands of Arab and Jew.
Reader, in writing this I become you, I must awake
in your darkness and mine and sleep with your sleep
and mine. As a stone I will not stone the innocent
or guilty, my Arabs and Jews will do
what my imagination wishes: make peace.
If You bring the flood, I will dam you up
as a river, though I do it on lined paper,
with an awkward hand. I believe something is thundering
in the mold, churning the hives of insects,
that the breath of every living creature mixes
in a kiss of life, that the killer's breath may taste of honey,
that when the forms of music change,
the walls of the city tremble.

THE ALTAR

One by one I lit the candles of nothingness,
a candle for each nostril, the eyes and ears,
a candle for the mouth, penis and anus.
Under the clouds of nothingness,
below the flaming particles of the universe,
I stood beside the nothing tree,
I ate my fill.

To God I swore nothing.
In the blood and fires of without
nothing was written. I heard the sermons of nothing
and I knew nothing had come, and would come again,
and nothing was betrayed.

I called prayer
the practice of attention. Nothing was
the balance of things contrary.
Disobedient, I did not make
the sacrifice of the lamb or the child.

My candelabrum was ablaze.

MON PÈRE, ELEGY FOR PAUL CELAN*

I

After his death, her blood was glass
that shattered within her, my mother could not bleed
or heal. Once in the moonlit snows of France
she offered his dark soul her breast.
Now for her night meal, she stares
at a little fish and vegetables
ladled out of being,
as if they were a family crucifix.
Her work: etchings she holds up
(the whorls of her fingertips stained by acid)
small, detailed views of mountains,
coastlines, complex clouds.
Sometimes you simply have to repeat
a little of the design of the creator—
nothing whatsoever made by man.

2

My father could turn the word being
into begging, into bed, into please,
his son twists his legs around his own neck,
man of rope, no farther from my father
than where a tree may root;
I hang by my teeth
from a rope fixed to the roof,
while the 19th-century French band below
plays "Art is the True Religion."
I bite a stranger's leather tongue.

---

* *The poet Paul Celan threw himself into the Seine in 1970; his son
is an aerialist and juggler.*

3

Juggler as poet, not the fire-eater,
not the fat man, like father, like son:
my chilly eyes and two hands keep three, four, ten,
twenty clubs or white plates going in air,
like after likes, the sins of the fathers,
red silk balls, kept up in the air.
I throw up household effects: his Hebrew Bible,
a yellowing toothbrush, shoes and ties,
his murdered family, his thanks
that it happened to them, not to him.
I fling up against the crowd
my father's head, red silk balls, white plates
of the unthinkable, a way of mourning,
Jerusalem remembered, synagogue as circus.
Prophecy has fallen to sleight of hand,
better to learn magic, better to change
two blue eggs in a lacquer box
into three fluttering white doves.

4

Hanging on by a hair,
on that night different
from all other nights,
he could not pull himself out
by a breath.
He was something like hair
with feeling only at its roots.

Coming from a musical family,
he could not bear to hear music,
he could not stop
his constant, endless bleeding
in private, in public,

on the bread he ate,
on my mother's face.
Drowning
sent his life and blood off
in water like smoke.
His fingers were dactyls again.

A fisherman found him
decomposing below
Notre Dame Cathedral.
They quickly washed their hands of him.
In the Chapel of Virtues
the Virgin wept for her son
surrounded by images
of women without lives:
Temperance, Fortitude, Justice,
and Prudence with her three eyes
to see past, present and future.

Once his garments were warmed
when Jehovah quieted the earth
with the south wind.
The language of the psalms
has a different word
for why asked in the past
and why asked in the future.
Why lose the rest of spring, mon père?

LINES FOR A STAMMERING TURKISH POET

To Edouard Roditi

I

When he was a child, he thought of sea birds as Muslim,
fidgety land birds as Christians and Jews;
in his village, when a man approached, the women
squatted down in the roadside and turned away,
the branches of pomegranate and orange trees
heavy with fruit, lowered to the ground . . .
In the sky-blue copybook of his school days
he was compelled by revolution to change
from an Arabic alphabet, with its gardens and forests,
to twenty-nine Roman letters bare as sticks.
Now he is older, the birds have no religion.
He walks the industrial gutters that cross the silk routes,
faithful to January, two-faced god of beginnings.
He speaks for, stammers for—mothers, mothers
and mothers, he gets tangled in four thousand years
of apron strings of the Hittite, Greek, Roman,
Christian mother Goddesses and ordinary
women who do most of the work.

He has come to a bridge, the tongue of a balance
that crosses the Bosphorus between Europe
and Asia. He says: "Although it seems for commerce
not wisdom, a br-br-br-br-bridge
across the meandering Bosphorus is a Goddess.
They fa-fa-fa-found her statue near Ephesus."
Her face had a beauty exceptional
even for a God—lady of wild things,
sister of Apollo, from her neck she wore
a wreath of eighteen bull's balls to show
the fear and love the Greeks had for her,
the kind of sacrifice she commanded.

2

In the agora of rusty girders and broken concrete
sheep graze among burning automobile tires.
At dawn, when Gods roll over in our human beds
and the sea mends the torn robes of the mother Goddess,
in mosques that were churches in Byzantium,
beneath the giant calligraphy of sacred names,
men without shoes, standing,
cup their hands behind their ears at the beginning
of prayer to better hear a voice before they touch
their foreheads to the ground, prostrate themselves.
Strengthened by years of his hatred, and hatred of hatred,
he says, stammering, "They are all covered with dust,
a kind of bone meal of those they have prayed to kill,
hoping to follow the green bird that leads to paradise."

3

He offers two souls, East and West, over coffee
like honey cakes to Muslims, Christians and Jews.
He writes his love poems in a fifteen-syllable
Greek line. Sweet-faced, bearded, sometimes jailed,
lonely Ottoman of extra syllables,
he sees downhill, above the dark river
long accustomed to slaughter,
the marble fragments of ancient tombstones,
the Jewish cemetery, an avalanche of broken writing.
Of course chaos is not separate from form,
above Istanbul exploding stars
may be an embroidered slipper
on the bare foot of the Asian night.
With only his tongue to know, he stammers,
"Wer—were words come without human intervention:
A word is a sacrificial goat
and the goat sent into the wilderness.
Sometimes my semen turns to blood."

DAYDREAM

In a daydream near the lake in Canada,
to save my dog, I fired a shotgun at a bear's head,
turning its face and eyes into bleeding peach pits.
Mama bear gasped something less than a syllable,
made for the forest like a shot,
stood up for a moment at the brambles
like my small son standing in bed asking "Why? Why?"
What can she teach her two cubs now? They are still hungry.
Not the lesson of acorns, not the song of grubs in damp stumps—
that mice are sweet. Once she nursed her cubs while she slept
two heartbeats per minute, under branches and fresh snow.
Now they tongue the blood from her face—
then they die in my cruel song.

THE PUBLIC GARDENS OF MUNICH

The park benches, of course, are ex-Nazis.
They supported the ass of the SS
without questioning; the old stamp *Juden Verboten*
has been painted out.
The only signs of World War II, photographs,
displayed at the classical Greek museum,
show its roof bombed, now handsomely repaired,
although the sculpture itself has been overcleaned
by a very rough hand.

But the flowers are the children of other flowers,
the hypocrite roses and the lying begonias,
part of gardens so sentimental, so ordered,
they have nothing to say about freedom and beauty,
nothing to say about the burning bush.
They should see the flowers on the hills of Judea,
pushing between limestone and gypsum, ordinary
beautiful flowers with useful Hebrew and Arabic names,
useful to children, old people, everyone,
their colors and grace, the poetry of them,
page after page.

A man can hide under his shirt
flowers made by metal and fire, stems cut,
neck wounds, missing bone, history
of generations, new branches grafted
onto old stumps.
The saying goes in the streets of Munich:
"Wear a good overcoat." Everyone knows,
you can put a dead body under a handkerchief.
Every handkerchief's a grave,
that's why so many gentlemen wear clean handkerchiefs
in their breast pockets. For the ladies, lace gloves

serve the same purpose—blue handkerchiefs, pink gloves,
green, lavender *und so weiter* are symbolic—
but you have to really know—white for Jew,
blue for Jew, green for Polack, pink for—
you'd better watch out, a little joke.

This year in the Spanish garden during Carnival
someone decapitated a donkey,
Renaissance symbol of the Old Testament,
or perhaps the meaning is, as the TV
commentary said: the donkey
stands for a fifteenth-century Jew,
or was it just *Kinderspiele*,
a game like this hee-haw.

Later in Italy, at the Hotel Stendhal, Parma,
I discovered my friend from Munich can sleep through anything,
a lesson he learned for life during the Allied bombings,
while I sleep four hours on, four hours off,
a lesson I learned in the U.S. Navy.
We still sleep at war. Awake, we embrace.

THE DECADENT POETS OF KYOTO

Their poetry is remembered for a detailed calligraphy
hard to decipher, less factual than fireflies in the night:
the picture-letters, the characters, the stuff
their words were made from were part of the meaning.
A word like "summer" included a branch of plum blossoms,
writing about "summer in a city street"
carried the weight of the blossoming branch,
while "a walk on a summer afternoon"
carried the same beautiful purple shade.

They dealt with such matters distractedly,
as though "as though" were enough, as though
the little Japanese woman with the broom
returning to her husband's grave to keep it tidy
was less loving than the handsome woman in the café
off the lobby of the Imperial Hotel
who kissed the inside of her lover's wrist.
In their flower arrangements, especially distinct
were the lord flower and emissary roses—

public representations now shadows.
Their generals and admirals took musicians
with them to war, certain their codes
would not be deciphered, in an age when hats
and rings were signs of authority and style.
They thought their secrets were impenetrable,
they thought they had the power to speak and write
and not be understood, they could hide the facts
behind a gold-leaf screen of weather reports.

It was Buddha who had an ear for facts:
coins dropping into the ancient cedar box,
hands clapping, the sound of temple bells and drums.

Codes were broken, ships sank, men screamed
under the giant waves, and a small hat
remained afloat longer than a battleship.

THE MISCARRIAGE

I

You had almost no time, you were something
not quite penciled in, you were more than darkness
that is shaped by its being and its distance from light.
(To give birth in Spanish is to give to light.)
There was the poetry of it:
a word, a letter changed perhaps
or missing and you were gone.
Every word is changed when spoken.
The beauty is you were mine and hers,
not like a house, a bed, a book, or a dog,
unsellable, unreadable, not love, but of love,
an of—with a certain roundness and a speck
that might have become an eye, might have
seen something, anything: light,
Tuscany, Montana, read Homer in Greek—
unnamed of, saved from light and darkness.

2

I was not told of you until long after,
I would not have handed down that suitcase
to her through the train window in Florence
had I known. I might have suggested tea
instead of Strega, might have fanned the air.
Fathers can do something. I didn't ask the right questions.
I did not offer any sacrifice.
I just walked around in my usual fog looking
at pictures of the Virgin impregnated by words.

What if the Virgin Mother had miscarried? What if
the Magi arrived with all that myrrh and frankincense
like dinner guests on the wrong evening?

Our Lady embarrassed, straightening up,
Joseph offering them chairs he made and a little wine,
sinners stoned in the street
while John who would have been called the Baptist
wept in his mother's belly.

THE INHERITANCE

In Canada, on a dark afternoon,
from a cabin beside Lake Purgatory
I saw your two clenched fists in a tree—
your most recent rage—until I came to my senses,
and saw two small lighted glass lamps reflected
through a window onto the maple leaves.
Was it simply that I had stolen away
in the wilderness to go fishing on your birthday,
twelve years after your death, and you
less than your rusty pliers in my fishing box?

It is late August in the moral North.
To answer your first question,
I obey the fish and game laws
of New York State, Ontario and Quebec.
The odd branch has already turned red.
As for me I have turned inside out,
I cry for revolution against myself—
no longer red, I'm parlor pink and gray,
you, less than a thumbprint on a page.

Matters still outstanding: you will not remember—
a boy, I cut school, sneaked out
to the 42nd Street library to read among readers
like a stray lion cub taken into a great pride.
I have kept your Greek grammar,
your 78 revolutions per minute
recording of Rossini's *Barber*
you played to stop me from crying,
almost my first memory.
Your "valuable papers," now valuable
only to me, I fed to a fire years ago.
Frankly I am tired of receiving letters from the dead

every day, and carrying you on my back,
out of the burning city,
in and out of the bathroom and bedroom,
you less than the smoke you wanted for a shroud.

Let us dance with Sarah behind the curtain
where God in his divine humor
tells Abraham Sarah will at ninety bear a son,
and she asks, laughing within herself, "Will I have pleasure?"
Take one foot, then the other . . . Imitate a departure
if you make it not, and each going
will lend a kind of easiness to the next.
Father, you poisoned my father.
I am standing alone, telling the truth
as you commanded. (Without too many
of the unseemly details, like the sounds of you in bed
sucking, I thought, on fruit I later would not eat.)
You, less than a seed of a wild grape.

Today, in the last moments of light
I heard a fish, a "Musky," your nickname, break water.
As I sing my song of how you
will be remembered, if I could
out of *misericordia*, I'd tie you to the mast
and stuff your ears with wax. I regret
some parts of the body forgive, some don't. Father,
do not forget your 18-inch Board of Education ruler
on which I measured my penis, marking its progress.

You kept it on your desk before you till your old age.
One reason, perhaps, for the archaic Greek smile
I wore on my face through boyhood.
I never thought I'd dig your grave with laughter.

NEW MOON

Full of the city and accounting, I stepped out of my car
into the mist and sand near the Atlantic,
to see a bright haze within a cloud,
a wordless passage from an older testament.
I had forgotten in the unreadable night
that once like a child learning to speak I tried to write,
on a dark night of my life, something lunar,
to be my own Ordinary of secrets and rebirth.

In my prayer book I find, after the blessings
called "The Giving Thanks for Trees Blossoming"
and "The Giving Thanks for Fragrance,"
prayers for the new moon in large type,
night prayers for unconscious sins and new beginnings,
to be read outside in moonlight or at an open window.
I speak of prayer, it is not prayer.
I count syllables like minutes before sunset.
I have nothing to show the new moon
but a few lines about the present,
the lesser time under the sun.
Old enough, I have learned to be my own child.
To get even, have I lived my life to make adults cry?
Tonight the child runs to and from me,
already full of memory and cruel history,
talking a blue streak about injustices.
The child falls asleep. I'm up late with the moon.
It is not revelation but the mystery itself I praise.

LETTER TO NOAH

Greetings, I hope you will not be disappointed I survived
the flood riding the back of a giant turtle. Adrift
in the waters of chaos, above the ice-covered mountain ranges
that had become part of the deep,
I saw the sun and moon embrace in terror.
I kept my senses counting the days that had no name,
I heard all manner of newborn things
crying for their mothers—the last living sounds.
We swam through islands of angry faces, an ocean of rodents
devouring each other, great serpents of children knotted
together in whirlpools. I saw the beauty of jungle birds
that in mid-afternoon filled the horizon like a sunset.
Once I saw your vainglorious ark, three stories of lights,
your windows filled with the riches of the world,
a woman on the deck, her wet blouse
clinging to her breasts—I was that close.
If you had heard my call, saw me alive,
would you have reached down to save me?
It wouldn't have been the end of the world.
But you of course were following orders, a tune as old
as Adam's song to Eve before the serpent.
Then after all the days of nights I heard my turtle gasp, "Hallelujah."
I turned and saw the rainbow, the raven and the dove,
in sunlight the waters that reflected nothing, receding,
Noah, I think I am as grateful for the rainbow as you.
I have survived, corrupt and unclean.

THE POOR OF VENICE

The poor of Venice know the gold mosaic
of hunger, the grand architecture of lice,
that poverty is a heavier brocade
than any doge would shoulder. To the winter galas
the poor still wear the red silk gloves of frostbite,
the flowing cape of chilblain.

The winged lion has his piazza, lame dogs
and pigeons with broken wings have theirs.
Let the pigeons perform for dry corn
their commedia dell'arte in the palms of tourists.
The rich and poor don't share a plate of beans.

There used to be songs about squid and sardines
in love the poor could make some money from.
A boy in bed with his family asks for a violin,
his father leaps up,
"Violin, violin, I'll buy you a shovel!"
Moored in the dark canals of Venice,
gondolas for prisoners, for the sick,
gondolas for the dying, the hungry,
tied to poles by inescapable knots
looped by Titian.

Salute an old Venetian after his work.
Eating his polenta without quail, he sits
on a slab in the freezing mist, looking back
at the lagoon and his marble city:
years of illusion, backache, sewerage and clouds.

THE HAWK, THE SERPENTS AND THE CLOUD

In writing, he moved from the word *I*,
the word once a serpent curled between the rocks,
to *he*, the word once a hawk drifting above the reeds,
back to *we*: a nest of serpents.
Of course the hawk attacked the serpents.
She became a cloud, nursed us, mothered us,
scrubbed us with rain. *I*, once a serpent, know the Chinese
character for *he* is a standing figure,
the sign for *she* is a kneeling figure,
the word *cloud* is formed by two horizontal waves above a plain,
and that in writing Chinese
you must show feeling for different parts of the word.
Writing contains painting and painting writing.
Each is bird and sky to the other, soil and flower.

THE LACE MAKERS

Their last pages are transparent: The Lace Makers
choose to see a world behind the words,
not the words, tatting, not stitching, an open page
of knots, never a closed fabric stitched by needles.
They see from the apples and pears on their plates
out to the orchard, from their tatting
to a bird with a piece of straw in his beak.
From combings transferred onto a running thread,
they make a row of rings resembling a reef,
a chain of knots, hammocks, fishnets,
things found in the hands of sailors.
Without looms, with their fingers,
they make bridal objects, knotted hairnets
seen in certain Roman bronze female portraits,
the twisted threads and knotted fringes of dusty
Egyptian wrappings, something for the cuff,
the lapel, the drawing room, nothing to wear in the cold.
They care about scrolls and variations,
a handkerchief, a design on a pillow,
a completed leaf, four ovals with connecting chains
becoming four peacocks, part of a second leaf,
as if they were promised the world would not
be destroyed, with or without paradise.

Noting the French for tatting is *frivolité*,
they make false chains, things obsolete, improper,
in search of new forms. They carry a thread
to a distant point, eight measured peacocks
of equal size with an additional thread
and the ends cut off. It has the heartless advantage
of being decorative in itself.
They sit and work in the aging light
like Achilles, hiding from his pursuers
in a dress, tatting among the women,

discovered by Odysseus who offered a trap of gifts:
the women picked hammered gold leaves and bracelets,
deserted by his Gods, Achilles chose a sword.
In any fabric there are constant beginnings
and endings with cut threads
to be finished off and cut out of sight.
The lacemakers read their yellow lace,
washing and ironing it is a fine art
—beautiful a straw basket filled with laundry
and language. But shall we call gossip prophecy?
Who will turn the hearts of the fathers to the children
and the hearts of the children to their fathers?
They are unworthy of undoing the laces of their own shoes.

THE GEOGRAPHER

Before the geography of flowers and fruit,
he learned warmth, breast, wetness.
He came late to mapmaking, the arches and vaults
of the compass, a real and unimagined world
of prevailing winds, coastlines and mountains,
large bodies of water, rifts and faults,
altitudes and depth. Under the stars
he studied what he learned as a child:
that geography determined history,
that weather defined places, principal products.
He would simply walk out of doors to find
the Jews of the wind arguing with the Jews of the dust:
who shall be placed among the writings,
who among the prophets, what is legend
and what is visionary dream.

He studied the deserts, the once dry Mediterranean,
the colossal sculptures of Egypt and Assyria,
art that outweathered its gods.
Under *History* his notes linked the Armada—
the entry: "parched Castile had nothing,
had to conquer the world"—to Napoleon leading his armies
into the Russian winter—like a carload of sheep
each marked for slaughter with a splash of red paint.
They too seemed to have a leader.
He believed the molecular connection of all living stuff
since the beginning of life made him less lonely—
no message, but a *cri de cœur*.

He had a small globe of the earth he kept
inside another blue and silver globe of stars.
He learned and relearned touch, flesh and place,
the simple "where is," the colors of nearness,

the light and dark of naked bodies in repose.
He learned countries and cities as if
they were verbs, meaning beyond subject:
the word poetry came from the Greek "to make,"
the Chinese character for poetry is "to keep."
A fine day does not forget lightning and thunder. Facts:
it was not the fifty-degrees-below-zero cold in winter,
or the ten-degrees-below-zero cold in summer,
that caused one percent of the population to die each day
in the coal and blood-black snows of the Soviet arctic.
Memory makes any place part illusion.
Weather remembers, has a long memory of itself,
oceans and landscape, nothing human.

He came to a certain calm in his studies:
the healing and destroying power of water,
the chaos of forest fires, followed by new unheard-of growth.
He noted bougainvillea and oleander
crossing continents like vacationing lovers—
he sketched the universe as an animal belly
full of exploding gases.
He had to make it all human as a bad joke.

He had cause to be frightened,
to turn his head to the beauty of it.
Under *Fruit trees of this world*, he wrote:
there's a murder for every apple, every peach, every pear,
beneath the oak a starving child for every acorn,
among the evergreens a lie for every pine needle.
These are the forbidden fruit.

THE DEBT

I

I owe a debt to the night,
I must pay it back, darkness for darkness
plus interest.
I must make something out of almost nothing,
I can't pay back by just not sleeping
night after night. I hear them screaming
in the streets of New York, "What? What? What?"

I can't write a check to the night,
or a promissory note: "I'll write songs."
Only the nightmare is legal tender.
I bribe owls, I appeal
to creatures of the night: "Help me
raccoons, catfish, snakes!"
I put my head in the tunnel of a raccoon,
pick up a fish spine in my mouth.
Perhaps the night will accept this?
Dying is my only asset.

These days driving along I turn up my brights.
I love and am grateful for anything that lights
the darkness: matches, fireworks, fireflies.
My friend who's been to Antarctica
tells me when the sun is high against the ice
you see the shadow of the earth.
The night after all is just a shadow . . .
The debt keeps mounting.
I try to repay something by remembering
my Dante, the old five and ten thousand lira notes
had Dante's face etched on the front.
(I bought that cheap.) Hard cash to the night
is finding out what I do not want to know
about myself, no facts acceptable,
a passage through darkness,

where the one I stop to ask "Why? What?"
is always myself, I cannot recognize.

2

If only I could coin nightmares:
a barnyard in Asia,
the last dog and cat betrayed, are no more.
A small herd of three-legged blind cows
still gives milk.
A pig with a missing snout, its face like a moon,
wades in a brook.
A horse, its mane burnt to cinders,
a rear hip socket shot off, tries to get up,
thrusting its muzzle into the dark grass.
A rooster pecks without a beak or a coxcomb.
A rabbit that eats stones, sips without a tongue,
runs without feet.
A ditch of goats, sheep and oxen
locked in some kind of embrace.
All move their faces away,
refuse the charity of man
the warrior, the domesticator.
I see a whale with eyes yards apart
swimming out of the horizon,
surfacing as if it were going to die,
with a last disassociated vision,
one eye at peace
peers down into the valleys and mountains
of the ocean, the other eye floats,
tries to talk with its lids to the multitude.
While in the great head
what is happening and what happened mingle,
for neither has to be.
I pray for some of my eyes to open and some to close.
It is the night itself that provides
a forgiveness.

4
Skull of Adam
&
The Wrong Angel

SAILING FROM THE UNITED STATES

In this country I planted not one seed,
Moved from address to address, did not plead
For justice in its courts, fell in love and out,
Thrust my arm into the sea and could not pull it out;
I did not see the summer lose its balance,
Or organize the lonely in a gang, by chance
I did not build a city or a ship, or burn
The leaves that fell last autumn, in my turn
Built by the numb city-building noise,
I learned the morning and the night are decoys
To catch a life and heap the profits of the grave.

I have lost a country, its hills and heroes;
In a country that taught me talk, confined
To the city of myself, I oppose
The marketplace and thoroughfares, my mind
Shaping this history, my mouth to a zero.
The wind in my house is not a wind through olive trees,
I hear no music in the janitor's keys,
I fashion no reed, no pipe, have not the wind for it,
My summer and winter prove counterfeit.
Through the villages of New England and the free country,
I will my unconditional mutiny,
I leave this crockery heaped on a shelf
For an old regime, to work myself
As a mine, subject to explosions and cave-in.

AND NOW THERE IS NO PLACE TO LOOK

And now there is no place to look,
there are no risks. Now we are familiar
with ourselves as unfamiliar things.

My mind spills, my hand wipes it away.
Beyond my reach the sea's gigantic snake
feeds upon itself, repeats the mind's play.

The fields grow dark with darkness that seems to be.
Our plans like burning matches in the wind.
Neither darkness nor light pass through me.

Through Italian cliffs, I have seen great caves,
where water enters for a thousand years,
makes one curve on rough stone—a pretty grave.

The wind has caught my shirt but who will steer?
Another night's debris floats the waves;
I hear the echo and what the echo hears.

THE GIFT

She gave me the gift of my own desire;
hollowed by fire as a tree
I have betrayed love for desire.

Gladly I would betray desire
but I cannot, until once more
love burns me through.

NICKY

She danced into the moonless winter,
a black dog.
In the morning when I found her
I couldn't get her tongue back in her mouth.
She lies between a Japanese maple
and the cellar door, at no one's feet,
without a master.

FOR JAMES WRIGHT

Hell's asleep now.
On the sign above your bed
nothing by mouth, I read *abandon hope*.

You sleep with your fist clenched,
your tongue and throat swollen by cancer,
make the sound of a deaf child
trying to speak, the smell
from the tube in your belly
is medicinal peppermint.

You wake speechless.
On a yellow pad your last writing
has double letters—two Zs and Ys in "crazy,"
you put your hand on your heart
and throw it out to me.
A few pages earlier you wrote,
"I don't feel defeated."

In your room without weather,
your wife brings you more days,
sunlight and darkness, another summer,
another winter, then spring rain.

When Verdi came to his hotel in Milan
the city put straw on the street
below his window
so the sound of the carriages
wouldn't disturb him—if I could,
I'd bring you the love of America.

I kiss your hand and head, then I walk out on you,
past the fields of the sick and dying,
like a tourist in Monet's garden.

LENIN, GORKY AND I

I

That winter when Lenin, Gorky and I
took the ferry from Naples to Capri,
nobody looked twice
at the three men having a lemon ice
in Russian wool suits hard as boards.
Behind us, a forgetful green sea,
and the Russian snows storming the winter palace.
We descended, three men a bit odd,
insisting on carrying our own suitcases
heavy with books: Marx, Hegel, Spinoza.
We took the funicular
up the cliffs of oleander and mimosa,
yet through the fumes of our cheap cigars
we observed how many travelers had come
to Capri with a beauty. Lenin to Gorky:
"In Moscow they'd kill on the streets for the girl
who showed me my room."
Within an hour of our arrival
we were sitting in the piazza drinking fizz,
longing for the girls strolling by:
a mother, a sister, a daughter.
You could smell an ageless lilac in their hair.
Lenin warned, raising our level from low to high,
"Love should be like drinking a glass of water . . .
You can tell how good a Bolshevik she is
by how clean she keeps her underwear."

2

It was then I split with the Communist Party.
Gorky welcomed the arrival of an old flame
from Cracow. Lenin bought white linen trousers
but would not risk the Russian Revolution
for what he called "a little Italian marmalade."
It was I who became the ridiculous figure,
hung up in the piazza like a pot of geraniums,
not able to do without the touch, taste and smell
of women from those islands in the harbor of Naples.

TRAVELS

I

In Barcelona I took a yellow cab up Jew Mountain
to a Golgotha of telephone poles,
I saw a horizon of lovers
suffering a hundred different deaths,
I saw time as a mother in the lap of her mother
give suck as women do in the beginning
—their hands made the wetness they touched.

I went into time and women like entering a cathedral:
madness to think sweating beauty needed me.
Above me, higher than the darkness,
stained glass windows told another story:
the speaking of the flesh, the *parlando*, the *hablar*.

What have women taught me, my beautiful teachers,
after all that lovemaking, that bathing?
How to read, dress and keep clean.
It is time to take on the inconveniences,
time to make and repair,
ways of kindness and deception,
ways to go to funerals and weddings—
toujours la tendresse.

2

It's a spring day near the Atlantic—
the sky as blue as her eyes,
time undresses before me,
moves like a girl
lifting her blouse over her head.
Now the quarrel really begins:
I tell her I have no complaints so far,
I'm not really speaking for myself—
that I don't want her to go.
I've seen the suffering she caused her lovers,
their utter humiliation.
Yes, old men and young boys,
old women and young girls.

Naked, she takes a mouthful of wine—
smiling her wicked rose-petal smile,
her eyes an endless intelligent blue,
she leans over me and from above
pushes the wine into my mouth—
then puts her hand to my lips
as if to tell me
I was saying the wrong thing.

CLOUD SONG

Working class clouds are living together
above the potato fields, tall white beauties
humping above the trees, burying their faces
in each other, clouds with darker thighs,
rolling across the Atlantic. West,
a foolish cumulus hides near the ocean
afraid of hurricanos.
Zeus came to the bed
of naked Io as a cloud,
passed over her and into her as a cloud,
all cloud but part of his face
and a heavy paw, half cloud, half cat
that held her down.
I take clouds to bed that hold me
like snow and rain, gentle ladies,
wet and ready, smelling of lilac hedges.
I swear to follow them like geese,
through factory smoke,
beyond the shipping lanes and jet routes.
They pretend nothing—opening, drifting, naked.
I pretend to be a mountain
because I think clouds like that.
A cloudy night
proclaims a condition of joy.
Perhaps I remember a certain cloud,
perhaps I bear a certain allegiance
to a certain cloud.

ON SEEING AN X-RAY OF MY HEAD

This face without race or religion
I have in common with humanity—
mouth without lips, jaws without tongue,
this face does not sleep when I sleep,
gives no hint of love or pleasure,
my most recent portrait smells of fixative
and rancid vinegar, does not appear
male or female.
I don't look as if I work for a living.

I will ask for fire. I can not risk
lovers, walking in a wood, turn up this face,
see such putrefaction they question
why they've come to lie on the grass,
picnic, fish or read to one another.
I will not have them find me staring
after their lovemaking,
under the leaves and branches of summer,
a reminder of mortality.

I prefer the good life, in real death
a useful skull to house small fish
or strawberries, a little company.
I must remember death is not always
a humiliation, life everlasting
is to be loved at the moment of death.
I hold my lantern head before me,
peer into one eye, see darkness, darkness
in the other, great funerals of darkness
that never meet.

APOCRYPHA

You lie in my arms,
sunlight fills the abandoned quarries.

I planted five Lombard poplars,
two apple trees died of my error,
three others should be doing better.
I prepared the soil,
I painted over the diseased apple tree,
I buried the available dead around it:
thirty trout that died in the pond
when I tried to kill the algae, a run-over raccoon,
a hive of maggots in every hole.
This year the tree flowered, bears fruit.
Are my cures temporary?

I chose abortion in place of a son,
because of considerations.

I look for the abandoned dead,
the victims, I shall wash them,
trim their fingernails and toenails.
I learn to say Kaddish,
to speak its Hebrew correctly,
a language I do not know,
should I be called upon.
I abandon flesh of my flesh
for a life of my choosing.

I take my life from Apocrypha.
Warning of the destruction of the city,
I send away the angel Raphael
and my son. Not knowing if I am right
or wrong, I fall asleep in the garden,

I am blinded by the droppings
of a hummingbird or crow.
Will my son wash my eyes with fish gall
restoring my sight?

You lie in my arms,
I wrestle with the angel.

THE MESSENGER

1

On the way to visit a physician,
a friend, who would soon suddenly die,
I saw a pigeon on a heap of rubble
standing more like a gull,
other pigeons in wild flight
searching the wreckage
of two Times Square theaters,
razed to build a hotel.
They were looking for their roof,
their nest, their young,
in the hollows of broken concrete,
in the pink and white dust,
they fluttered around the wrecking ball
that still worked the façade,
the cornice of cement Venetian masks.

2

I'll be no messenger for pigeons.
I can not help but see
how like their markings—
the yellow, red and blue dots
that speckle the trout and butterfly.
The roof, a giant bird of tar paper,
takes its last breaths on the broken stage.
There are no tragic pigeons.
I mourn my sweet friend
fallen among the young,
unable to sustain flight,
part of the terrible flock,
the endless migration
of the unjustly dead.

3

When I was a child, before I knew the word for love
or snowstorm, before I remember a tree or a field,
I saw a white bird in a blizzard, huddled in snow
and ice on our kitchen window sill.
My first clear memory of terror.

4

This winter I hung a gray and white stuffed
felt seagull from the ring of my window shade,
a reminder of good times by the sea,
of Chekhov and impossible love.
It pleased me the gull
sometimes lifted a wing in the drafty room.
Once when looking at the gull I saw
through the window a living seagull glide
toward me then disappear—what a rush of life!
I remember its hereness, while in the room
the senseless symbol, little more than a bedroom slipper,
dangled on a string.

5

My childhood hangs like a gull in the distant sky.
Its eyes behind mud and salt
see some dark thing below:
on a trawler off Montauk
I am heading home cleaning my catch,
seagulls dive close, desperate for the guts.
A little above the Atlantic we race toward port,
their different struggling faces inches from mine.
I feed, they take. I feed, they take.
For a few minutes I am part of the flock.

VOMIT

The stomach and the heart can be torn
out through the mouth if you get the right hook.
Because puking I was held up to this world,
because I have lived, burped in my mother's arms,
it comes out now:
what I thought I had swallowed, matters settled,
understood, kept out of mind—our father,
who keeps us in the speeding car,
who will not stop, let me puke in the grass
where it will hardly be noticed,
among the weeds and roadside flowers.

I throw up on myself the half-digested
meat and salad of what I devoured
in pleasure, the perfectly seasoned
explanation of love and social forces
that made me feel slightly superior.

I put my finger down my throat
so I can become part of this world,
I refuse to hear voices that speak to me
in rage without sense,
because my body and soul are locked
in secret battle, because the soul is voiceless
while the body can speak, gasp, sing, whisper,
utter what it pleases, because the body
becomes what it consumes and the soul
refuses such fires;
because the devil says
vomit is the speech of the soul.

I give the devil his due,
because the soul's speech is so rare,
to hear it
I must listen out of earshot,
I must give myself like a lover
and take like a lover, resisting and giving
till the heart is hooked and pulled out.

SHIT

I've been taught my daily lesson,
that man shall squat alone in secret,
I've been taken off my high horse,
I've bent down,
interrupted my day to humble myself,
no need to fall on my knees.
With a genuflection of the gut,
I hunt where my bones stink.

Out of the pain of this world
a kindness, a shape each of us
learns by heart: moon crescent,
jewelweed, forget-me-not,
hot lava. Christ, is this
the ghost in everything,
what I can and cannot,
I will and will not,
I have and have not,
what I must and must not,
what I did and did not?
An infant gasps in ecstasy,
tears of shit drip from a man
who cannot cry.

Most men near death cannot withhold,
they shit on themselves
when what they are
is all out of them:
wind, kindness, cruelty
all done, left behind,
when they must be changed
and cannot remember
who chose to soil us,
who makes us clean.

SNOT

I cannot forget the little swamp
that grows in my head,
cousin of the tear,
snot, my lowly, not worthy of sorrow,
the body's only
completely unsexual secretion.
No one my dears is hot for snot
or its institutions: catarrh,
asthma, the common cold, although
I've heard "snot-nose" used to mean "darling"
or "my son." There's beauty in it,
familiar as the face of any friend.
Dogs eat it, no one gets rich on it.

FROG

I hold this living coldness,
this gland with eyes, mouth, feet,
shattered mirror of all creatures,
pulsing smile of fish, serpent and man,
feet and hands come out of a head
that is also a tail,
just as I caught him most of my life ago
in the sawdust of the icehouse.
I could not believe in him if he were not here.
He rests my spirit
and is beautiful as waterlilies.
The sound of his call is too large for his body:
"irrelevant, irrelevant, irrelevant."
Once in the dry countries he was a god.

AN EXCHANGE OF HATS

I will my collection of hats,
straw the Yucatan, fez Algiers 1935,
Russian beaver, Irish fisherman's knit,
collapsible silk opera, a Borsalino,
to a dead man,
the Portuguese poet, my dear Fernando,
who, without common loyalty,
wrote under seven different names
in seven different styles.
He was a man of many cafés,
a smoker and nonsmoker.
His poets came to live in Lisbon,
had different sexual preferences,
histories and regional accents.

Still their poems had a common smell
and loneliness that was Fernando's.
His own character
was to him like ink to a squid,
something to hide behind.
What did it matter, writing in Portuguese
after the First World War? The center was Paris,
the languages French and English.

In Lisbon, workers on the street corner were arguing
over what was elegance, the anarchist manifesto,
the trial of Captain Artur Carlos de Barros
found guilty of " advocating circumcision"
and teaching Marranos no longer to enter church
saying, "When I enter I adore neither wood nor stone
but only the Ancient of Days who rules all."
The Portuguese say
they have the "illusion" to do something,

meaning they very much want to do it.
He could not just sit in the same café
wearing his own last hat, drinking port
and smoking *Ideals* forever.

LINGERING

I lie in your lap like a book.
I can tell a tale of base and divine crevices,
of wordless places, unreachable ledges,
high waterfalls, clouds, dropping down
to swamp lands.
I lingered on the footpaths in gardens
of oleanders and lemon trees,
but my flesh was torn and I tore flesh.
Solo I dangled, whimpered, wept, begged.
I have fathered and mothered, poisoned the nipple,
I offered fruit I would never eat.
I slipped into the furthest valley,
places without ornament:
deserted barracks.
I commanded a territory. I am Goliath,
a child has flung a stone into my head.

LOST POEM

Time has appetite
For milk and meat. Man is good eating,
Smeared with sex that he himself has fed upon
Like the sow the slop of the trough,
And the humming bird its flower.
The light itself stunned and entertained.
Love a human being? Anyone in his right mind
Would sooner lie down with a river or a tree.
I will no longer say that man is meat,
Or night and day is bread for a God.
There is wheat in the fields, a little of it for the starving.
Because beauty belongs to no one,
You lie in my arms and I am a thief.

MECOX BAY

On a bright winter morning
flights of honking geese
seem a single being
like the sky itself.
When my kind comes into such formation
I watch for firing squads.
I never saw a line of praying figures take flight.
On an Egyptian relief I've seen
heads of prisoners
facing the same direction,
tied together by a single rope
twisted around each neck
as if they were one prisoner.
Again the honking passes over my roof.
A ridiculous, joyous bird
rises out of my breast, joins the flock,
but I am left on earth with my kind.
They tie us throat to throat down here.
After a poem, I *hoonnk hoonnk . . . hoonnk.*

CLOWN

I

He lived in flight from an apartment,
desolate as Beethoven's jaw. On the go
he could put his own life aside as an actor,
he drank till his feet turned purple
or into goat hooves. He could play the serpent,
Eve, Adam, the apple before or after it was bit.
He wandered beside himself, a figure far from himself
as orange rind: he could turn from David into Saul weeping—
to Absalom, his hair caught in a tree. He could play his own fool,
his own column of cloud, the presence of God.
He could throw himself out into the garbage,
or, like a child's top on a string,
turn red and blue then whirl into a single color.
He played a Buddhist priest reading from his Book
into the ear of a corpse who hears
the reader's voice telling him all these visions
are his own unrealized, undiscovered forms,
the horrible furies and the calm
he must come to understand are his.

2

"Far below the salt cliffs," he wrote in his Book of Hymns,
"the river's tongue has emptied into the sea."
Only the man-bird flies from the Dead Sea to the Himalayas,
from the ancient dead shrouded in poetry
to the never-ending ice so thick, the dead
are ritually butchered and fed to vultures that,
surrounded by haloes of the sun, rise like doves
out of the jeweled snow. In the glacial silence
a man's leg-bone makes a sweeter whistle than your ram's horn.

3

To bathe at birth, marriage and death, "a rule in Tibet,"
was not enough for him. "No one has ever slid down
the Himalayas so fast," he said in a coarse aside.
Unteachable, he learned, he fell
more like Richard II than Adam.
In a farce he came closest to the stinking breath
of his own mortality, trying to lift a snapping turtle off a busy road,
it bit into his shoe, he fell back out of the blue—
broke his ankle and elbow.

4

What did he know that no one knew?
The care he wanted to give, that no one else would give.
He had lived to sing to his dying mother
from her bedside. Now memory is his mother,
she keeps his life from burning off like a morning mist.
One black tear painted at the corner of his right eye,
a red tear at the left,
he wept over a glass of spilled milk. He pretended
to play Mozart on a violin without lessons.
He bought himself a fiddle and a bow
strung with circus-horse hair, an earthly bow, not a rainbow.
Who was he to know so many tunes?
He just played his everyday music—
he would never wrap the letters of the holy name
around his fingers. He wrote a song that began:
"I fall back from making love
to the kind of day it is . . ."

ELEGY FOR MYSELF

The ashes and dust are laughing, swaddled,
perfumed and powdered, laughing at the flowers,
the mirrors they brought to check his breath,
and he no longer singular.
Who will carry his dust home in merriment?
These things need a pillow, a wife,
a dog, a friend. Plural now he is all the mourners
of his father's house, and all the nights and mornings too.
Place him with "they love" and "they wrote,"
not "he loves" and "he writes." It took so much pain
for those S's to fly off. It took so much trouble
to need a new part of speech. Now he is
something like a good small company of actors;
the text, not scripture, begins, "Who's there?"

THE HANGMAN'S LOVE SONG

In the house of the hangman
do not talk of rope,
useless death, half death,
little death; the victim
always hangs himself,
trap sprung, tongue ripped
like love in the house.
Despite the world's ways,
I want a useful funeral.
High, on tiptoe,
swinging back
and forth, the victim,
who cannot speak,
mimics the bell,
such things as bait
for wild game, and love.
Brain hung and heart,
hope swings, sun creaks,
rope in the wind,
and the hangman sings.

DULCIE

I fly the flag of the menstruating black dog:
a black dog dripping blood over us all.
My flag barks, licks your face,
my flag says, "I am alive, willing,
part of the natural order of things.
You are a supernatural creature."

I walk across the road to the stream.
In a rush of water—something surfaces
—I hold my dog back.
A snake has caught a trout by the vent,
lifts the fish out of the water. The snake's head
cuts a line through the shaded water
into the sunlight,
crosses the stream to a ledge of gravel and jewelweed.
The trout is held into the summer air,
its brightest colors already begun to fade.
The snake uncoils, begins to devour the fish
head first.

The trees remembering my mother
kiss me, because she told me:
be the sweet dog that licks the face and washes the feet
of the bum passed out in the park
—she caught a seed flying over a city street,
put it in her glove,
took it home and planted it.
I sprawl with my dog on the floor
of all-night restaurants
because the entire shape of time
is a greater, more ferocious beast
than anything in it.

THE RETURN

It was justice to see her nude haunches
backing toward me again after the years,
familiar as water after long thirst.
Now like a stream she is, and I can lie beside
running my hand over the waters, or sleep;
but the water is colder, the gullies darker,
the rapids that threw me down have shallowed;
I can walk across.

A SKETCH OF NEGRO SLAVES, PRISONERS IN CONCENTRATION CAMPS AND UNHAPPY LOVERS

The survivors have something in common—
captured by superior forces of violence,
probably in the middle of the night,
dumped into slave ship, boxcar or bed,
the smell of urine and feces in their nostrils,
the useless are directed by a finger
to the right, the useful to the left—
examined naked. They cannot worship
their own God or the God of their masters.
The "old-timers" become like children, they steal,
inform, giggle, learn to seem not there,
not to do anything extraordinary
like whistling or talking. They grow proud
of how smartly they stand at attention,
come to believe the rules
set down from above are desirable,
at least in camp or bed. They climb for air
over bodies and faces, dig their teeth
and fingernails into flesh and the brick ceiling,
trying to escape suffocation.
I thumb through files of photographs. Among Litvaks,
Gypsies, Poles and queers I find my likeness.

TWO FISHERMEN

My father made a synagogue of a boat.
I fish in ghettos, cast toward the lilypads,
strike rock and roil the unworried waters;
I in my father's image: rusty and off hinge,
the fishing box between us like a covenant.
I reel in, the old lure bangs against the boat.
As the sun shines I take his word for everything.
My father snarls his line, spends half an hour
unsnarling mine. Eel, sunfish and bullhead
are not for me. At seven I cut my name for bait.
The worm gnawed toward the mouth of my name.
"Why are the words for temple and school
the same?" I asked, "And why a school of fish?"
My father does not answer. On a bad cast
my fish strikes, breaks water, takes the line.

Into a world of good and evil, I reel
a creature languished in the flood. I tear out
the lure, hooks cold. I catch myself,
two hooks through the hand,
blood on the floor of the synagogue. The wound
is purple, shows a mouth of white birds;
hook and gut dangle like a rosary,
another religion in my hand.
I'm ashamed of this image of crucifixion.
A Jew's image is a reading man.
My father tears out the hooks, returns to his book,
a nineteenth-century history of France.
Our war is over:
death hooks the corner of his lips.
The wrong angel takes over the lesson.

SEPTEMBER EVENING

In late September on a school day
I take my father, failing, now past seventy,
to the rowboat on the reservoir; the waters
since July have gone down two hundred yards
below the shoreline.
The lake stretches before us—a secret,
we do not disturb a drifting branch, a single hawk.
For a moment nothing says, "thou shalt not."
If I could say anything to the sky and trees
I'd say things are best as they are.

It is more difficult for me to think
of my father's death than my own.
He casts half the distance he used to.
I am trying to give him something,
to stuff a hill between his lips.
I try to spoon-feed him nature, but an hour
in the evening on the lake doesn't nourish him,
the walk in the woods that comforts me
as it used to comfort him makes him shiver.
I pretend to be cold.

We walk back along the drying lake bottom,
our shoes sink into the cold mud—
where last spring there was ten feet of water,
where in early June I saw golden carp
coupling on the surface. It's after dark,
although I can barely see
I think I know where the fence is.
My father's hands tremble like the tail of a fish
resting in one place. As for me?
I have already become his ghost.

WINTER IN VERMONT

Where is the green, the revolutionary?
What good can come of snow and slate?
Vermont or father, what's my theme?
I eye the skin of a woodchuck
left hanging on barbed wire.
A stream moves under a foot of ice.
I read the last words of Henry Adams:
"My child keep me alive."

JANE'S GRANDMOTHER

Near her 104th year, light as a sparrow
she sits on a burnished leather Davenport,
the kind you can't slump in.
Her death is almost lost,
a comb that keeps her hair in place.
The rivers are older than she is.
In Montana the clouds are younger—
there's not much standing between anything
and the sky—the darkness older,
some trees older, the great withstanders.
Barbed wire runs from U.S. 6
into her fingers and arms.
Her daughters care for her fingernails,
brown shell of box turtle.
Honest homesteader, she still loves a kiss.
Her smile moves to the rings of a tree,
her daughters' faces and their daughters'.

SUMMER DAY

My face leans to touch
things fallen through blades of grass,
things too small to pick up between my fingers:
flecks of stem, petals, edge of husk,
—my brothers and sisters of no consequence.

I hear the panda's song,
on lonely afternoons
he strips bamboo with a false thumb,
uooh, uooh,
an inefficient contraption, part of his wrist,
while his real thumb is committed,
uooh, uooh,
for evolutionary and historical reasons,
to other work, mostly running and clawing,
uooh.

Neither lover nor patriot there is a cricket,
err, err,
that left in Puerto Rico
lives out its days,
err,
that dies if moved, *err,*
off its sugarcane island,
to Santo Domingo, Curaçao or Florida.
Err...... uooh, uooh,
small matters the law does not correct,
uooh, err, err.

POEM BEFORE MARRIAGE

I am part man, part seagull, part turtle.
What remains? I have a few seasons
of vanity and forty years in the muddy lake.
I float on the reservoir in Central Park,
my gull eyes, man flesh, turtle mouth, tear the water
hunting shadows of fish that never appear.
I live on things a great city
puts in a small bowl for emergencies.
I "Caw Caw," wishing the shell on my back
were a musical instrument.
I have already been picked out of the mud
three times and thrown
against apartment house walls, left for dead.

Jane, in my bed you will find feathers
and fragments of shell. When, swallowing darkness,
I have a nightmare in your arms, my eyes
film over, let me sink to the bottom
of the artificial lake.

Fish for me.

SWEET QUESTIONS

Why does she pick only the smallest wildflowers?
The daisy and daylily aren't gross,
lilacs, peonies and roses
are not base company.
Why are they so small, the wildflowers
she brings me,
the most delicate, purest of color?
What is their purpose
brought by her hand to the hand of her lover?

MORNING

Usually I wake
to a dreamlike landscape,
face outside my window—
the Atlantic, a Catskill stream,
or the lake in Central Park.
My breath stares,
my tongue regards,
I whisper in my wife's ear,
"Are you up?"
Some voices can see,
some see for others, change the world.
All my voice can do is sleep near her ear,
while she chooses to sleep or wake.

PRAYER FOR ZERO MOSTEL

Señor, already someone else,
O my clown,
the man in your image
was a bestiary,
sweet as sugar,
beautiful as the world,
lizard sitting on a trellis
follows blonde into john,
now he is a butterfly on the edge
of a black-eyed susan
—rhinoceros
filing down his own horn
for aphrodisiac.
Señor, already someone else,
a band of actors under bombardment
played Shakespeare,
the last days
of the Warsaw ghetto,
a few of the survivors
who crawled through the sewers
heard the SS was giving out visas
for America
at a certain hotel,
went to apply.
If you love life
you simply can't believe
how bad it is.
Señor, someone else,
a Yahweh clown,
iambic rectal thermometer of the world.
Farewell art of illusion,
playing yourself as a crowd.

THE MEETING

It took me some seconds as I drove toward
the white pillowcase, or was it a towel
blowing across the road, to see what it was.
In Long Island near sanctuaries
where there are still geese and swans,
I thought a swan was hit by an automobile.
I was afraid to hurt it. The beautiful creature
rolled in sensual agony,
then reached out to attack me.
Why do I feel something happened on the road,
a transfiguration, a transgression,
as if I hadn't come to see what was,
but confronted the white body,
tried to lift, help her fly,
or slit its throat.
Why did I need this illusion,
a beauty lying helpless?

SQUALL

I have not used my darkness well,
nor the Baroque arm that hangs from my shoulder,
nor the Baroque arm of my chair.
The rain moves out in a dark schedule.
Let the wind marry. I know the creation
continues through love. The rain's a wife.
I cannot sleep or lie awake. Looking
at the dead I turn back, fling
my hat into their grandstands for relief.
How goes a life? Something like the ocean
building dead coral.

SIGN ON THE ROAD

1

The Atlantic a mile away is flat.
I rent this summer in Amagansett;
I see bayberries and pines. A one-eyed hound
Visits. Nothing is very far from the ground,
This is potato country, yellow and white
Blossom barely. Above the gravel pit
It is hardly wild. I find a snake skin
Pressed into the asphalt. I use tin
Roofing to scrape it up, and throw deep
Into a field the pearl leather. I keep
The tin to paint my sign MOSS in red,
Lean it on a fence where worms have fed;
I make my own target, throw my stone,
I nail my name down into my bone,
It falls in grass, I pick it up again
Like a sock-apple sweetened in the ditch.
I hope my sign will stand against the pitch
Of summer rain; crash in Atlantic hurricanes,
Drumming my name that creaks and grinds,
above the ditch on a piece of tin colder than the wind.

2

My friends, Moss is on the fence in Long Island,
The sea, a distance away like a grandfather
At a family reunion, says it's all sand.
But Moss is on the fence; it might as well
Be charged with high voltage, or painted blue
For all the good that will come of that.
It is a fact and if I scrape my name off
With a knife, the wood is wet underneath,
Just as sand is moist when you kick it up.
I suppose something like this wetnesss and the sun

Made the first living thing, the first sub-roach
That danced its way from under dead matter.
In the beginning before darkness was there a death?
Of course the wind or a telephone call
Moves the earth a little. Damn little.
The apple falls like an apple, and leaves
Hit the earth in their leafy way, and Moss
Shall be no exception. One fine day
I shall fall down like myself in a prison of anger.
Any day is a good day to be born.
I obey the orders of trees.
Moss is on the fence in Amagansett.

LOT'S SON

Three in his arms we sleep, Lot lies awake
All night, he does not let me lie awake
Or cut my own meat. All night
Through my ribs, I feel his body's heat.
He will not let me drink from a bright cup
(Unless he wash it), or climb high up.
His game: he points a finger at my eye
Saying, "You are crying," until I cry,
To make me a man. Rope, he holds me taut,
He knots, undoes the knots, I am caught
Round myself. A knot ties mother to son
Not father to daughter; all rope, but Lot,
Lot who tied us together is undone.

CLAMS

Ancient of Days, bless the innocent
who can do nothing but cling,
open or close their stone mouths.
Out of water they live on themselves
and what little sea water they carry with them.
Bless all things unaware that perceive
life and death as comfort or discomfort:
bless their great dumbness.

We die misinformed
with our mouths of shell open.
At the last moment, as our lives fall off,
a gull lifts us, drops us on the rocks, bare
because the tide is out. Flesh sifts the sludge.
At sea bottom, on the rocks below the wharf,
a salt foot, too humble to have a voice,
thumps for representation, joy.

PHOTOGRAPHY ISN'T ART

1

If I gave up the camera
or really made myself into a camera
or into a photograph,
if the sight of that photograph
made me change my life,
if I really held my darkest self
up to the light,
where life cannot be violated
by enlargers, light meters—
what creature would such changes keep alive?

My work changes color because of the work
like the hands of people handling coins.
The pregnant black woman
I saw during the blackout in New York City
carrying a refrigerator on her back
was not only a likeness.
Visions hide more than they reveal.

2

If I could really become a blur,
if I became for the joy of it—say a photograph
taken in a forgiving light
of the guests seated around the table
at Delacroix's dinner party, Paris, 1857,
when he had just made an omelette
so beautiful no one would eat it—
then if they called me to join at table
that company of poets and painters,
I would sweep the skull of Adam off the cloth,
smile for the photographer,
give thanks and suggest
we eat the omelette while it's still hot.

RETURN FROM SELLING

I comply with these disorders to give
myself food and lodging, a wanderer's hope
of inn or friendship, return to room
like a starfish out of its element,
not a man back from fields; I wash my hands,
rest my eyes as astronomers at dawn,
lie with no fewer turnings of my head
than men scanning Homer or charts of seas.
I exchange day for a room, the room for night,
and briefest thoughts of people still aloof,
common among these city rooms as sleep.

I look back to Greece and Assyria,
forward to the wall, back to the mind's wall
become a fortress, corrupting its kingdom
with idle craftsmen and shouts of selling at the gate,
walls keeping back neither ooze of Africa
nor the Arctic's superfluous snow,
nor will I be made traitor to love's loyalty
by the empty bed that informs against me;
nor will I forget the angel smiling in the doorknob.

WAR BALLAD

(after the Russian)

The piano has crawled into the quarry. Hauled
In last night for firewood, sprawled
With frozen barrels, crates and sticks,
The piano is waiting for the axe.

Legless, a black box, still polished;
It lies on its belly like a lizard,
Droning, heaving, hardly fashioned
For the quarry's primordial art.

Blood red: his frozen fingers cleft,
Two on the right hand, five on the left,
He goes down on his knees to reach the keyboard,
To strike the lizard's chord.

Seven fingers pick out rhymes and rhythm,
The frozen skin, steaming, peels off them,
As from a boiled potato. Their schemes,
Their beauty, ivory and anthracite,
Flicker and flash like the great Northern Lights.

Everything played before is a great lie.
The reflections of flaming chandeliers—
Deceit, the white columns, the grand tiers
In warm concert halls—wild lies.

But the steel of the piano howls in me,
I lie in the quarry and I am deft
As the lizard. I accept the gift.
I'll be a song for Russia, I'll be
an étude, warmth and bread for everybody.

THE GENTLE THINGS

I have had enough of Gods
And disaster;
The gentle things,
All loved ones survive,
Water survives in water,
Love in love.

I lie! The dead stain
Only themselves,
The wolf tears at the world,
Says, nothing is:
And the wolf is not the wind,
Is death's fingernail.

Dampness to dampness,
Had I been given
Only life's issue,
Not the song, or the silence
After the singing,
I should be content.

POTATO SONG

Darkness, sunlight and a little holy spit
don't explain an onion with its rose windows
and presentiment of the sublime,
a green shoot growing out of rock
or the endless farewells of trees.
Wild grasses don't grow just to feed sheep,
hold down the soil or keep stones from rolling;
they're meant to be seen, give joy, break the heart.
But potatoes hardly have a way of knowing.
They sense if it is raining or not,
how much sunlight or darkness they have,
not which wind is blowing or if there are dark clouds
or red-winged blackbirds overhead.
They are not aware if there are soldiers in the field
or not, moles or underground humpings.
Potatoes do not sleep, but must find pleasure
in their flowering. Sometimes
I hear them call me "mister" from the ditch.
Workers outside my window in Long Island
cut potatoes in pieces, bury them, water them.
Each part is likely to sprout and flower.
No one so lordly as not to envy that.

THE GARDEN

1

Since they were morose in August,
a hundred years old,
I thought the junipers not worth saving,
like useless old men.
I paid to have them torn out,
trunk and root. The roots had enough strength
to pull the truck back down so hard
the wheels broke the brick walk.

Heaped in front of my house,
cousins of the tree of mercy,
the dry gray branches
that did not suffer but had beauty to lose,
a touch of new growth.
Damp roots, what do I know
of the tenderness of earth,
the girlish blond dust?
Wrong, I dragged the junipers to the cliff,
and pushed them into the sea.
Then I put in my garden.

2

Go in darkness
is the command. Executioner,
I cared for the garden
not wanting to speak
of the suffering I have caused.
Sacred and defiled,
my soul is right
to deal with me in secret.

PRAYER

Give me a death like Buddha's. Let me fall
over from eating mushrooms Provençale,
a peasant wine pouring down my shirt-front,
my last request not a cry but a grunt.
Kicking my heels to heaven, may I succumb
tumbling into a rosebush after a love
half my age. Though I'm deposed, my tomb
shall not be empty; may my belly show above
my coffin like a distant hill, my mourners come
as if to pass an hour in the country,
to see the green, that old anarchy.

PLUMAGE

Off Montauk speedway I watch a swan
clam-gray in the remnant marsh, surrounded
by yesterday's swollen bread; jabbed, he attacks
the stick and an old automobile tire,
like great adversaries—moves out of reach,
trumpeting at the stone-throwing rabble.

Those ancient kisses, those first days were best,
my flesh in cloud almost moved the world.
Did I survive that first winter, first deceit?
For fifteen years my mind: a bird that would
not fly south—something like a swan circling
one place, refusing shelter.

I stand in the reeds under faded cloud.
All that plumage, the pomp of generations
in my wings, push back the mob:
the mercenary cold, the perjuring snows.
Lady, this summer when the world beckons,
I shall follow; next winter I shall go south.

LOVERS

We are gravel in the riverbed.
Years set us together in a bed of clay.
The river passes over us like suffering,
spring rains wash out the pine saplings,
in loneliness great trees sweep downstream—
avalanche, falling shale, water becomes mud,
becomes rock, willows root, startled trout
rest and spawn upon us,
a fisherman may push his boot
into our throats.

We know there are mountains:
we see them above the waters
as a single purple, blue and white blossom.
The river has changed course, leaving its bed.
What can I bring you,
facing the moon and the mountain?
We are used to seeing water,
then the moonlight on the surface of the water,
then the night, finally the moon itself.
The world comes, offers bread and fish,
not stone and serpent.

KANGAROO

My soul climbs up my legs,
buries its face in blood and veins,
locks its jaws on the nipple that is me.
I jump my way into the desert.
What does my soul, safe in its pocket, care
what I say to desert flowers?
Like a kangaroo
I pray and mock prayer.

I never took a vow of darkness.
I sit beside a boulder writing
on yellow lined paper. Once I thought
I'll pull my soul out of my mouth,
a lion will sleep at my feet,
I'll spend forty days in the desert,
I'll find something remarkable, a sign:
strains of desert grass
send the root of a single blade
down thirty feet.
I remember flakes of dry blood,
the incredible rescue of the man by the soul.

Under the aching knuckles of the wind,
move down in your pocket
away from remorse and money.
Learn discomfort from the frog,
the worm, the gliding crow,
they all hunt in repose, like men in prayer.
I can hardly distinguish myself from darkness.
I am not what I am. I demand the heart
to answer for what is given. I jump into the desert,
a big Jew, the law under my arm like bread.

OLD

The turtles are out,
loners on the road listening for mud,
old people looking for money.
Father, too old for hope,
when trees are burned black with cold,
what belongs to man, and what to nature?

With a penknife you used to make
ashtrays of turtles,
scrape out the living flesh—
gifts for friends,
now mine to take home if I want to.
A shell of your old self,
I want to whisper to you
the prayers and psalms you never taught me.
I never learned a healthy disrespect.
On my table I keep a bronze turtle—
a handle torn from an African sword,
a symbol of destroyed power.

The turtles move under the snow
in the dead of winter, under the loam,
chewing and scratching into frozen sand,
deeper than moles or grubs,
far from the loneliness of sunlight and weather.
I offer my hand, a strange other element.

THE LESSON OF THE BIRDS

The *Birds* of Aristophanes taught me
before there was sky or earth or air,
before there was mystery or the unknown,
darkness simply entered from darkness and departed
into darkness: it moved back and forth as the sea does,
all shells, grottos and shorelines that were to be
were darkness.

Time weathered such things,
had a secret heavy underwing;
an urge toward a warm continuum,
its odor of nests made a kind of light.
Before there was pine, oak or mud, seasons revolved,
a whirlwind abducted darkness, gave birth,
gave light to an egg. Out of the egg of darkness
sprang love the entrancing, the brilliant.
Love hatched us commingling, raised us
as the firstlings of love. There was never
a race of Gods at all until love
had stirred the universe into being.

THE VALLEY

Once I was jealous of lovers.
Now I am jealous of things that outlast us—
the road between Route 28 and our house,
the bridge over the river,
a valley of second-growth trees.
Under the birches, vines
the color of wolves survive a winter ten below,
while the unpicked apples turn black
and the picked fruit is red in the basket.
I am not sure that the hand of God
and the hand of man ever touch,
even by chance.

GOD POEM

I

Especially he loves
his space and the parochial darkness.
They are his family, from them grow his kind:
idols with many arms and suns that fathered
the earth, among his many mirrors, and some
that do not break:
rain kept sacred by faithful summer grasses,
fat Buddha and lean Christ, bull and ram,
horns thrusting up his temple and cathedral—
mirrors, but he is beyond such vanities.
Easy to outlive
the moment's death having him on your knees—
grunting and warm he prefers wild positions:
he mouths the moon and sun, brings his body
into insects that receive him beneath stone,
into fish that leap as he chases,
or silent stones that receive his silence.
Chivalrous and polite, the dead take
his caress, and the sea rolling under him
takes his fish as payment and his heaps of shells.

2

As he will,
he throws the wind arch-backed on the highway,
lures the cat into moonlit alleys,
mountains and fields with wild strawberries.
He is animal,
his tail drags uncomfortably, he trifles
with the suck of bees and lovers, so simple
with commonplace tongues—his eyes ripple
melancholy iron and carefree tin,

his thighs are raw from rubbing,
cruel as pine, he can wing an eagle off a hare's spine,
crouch with the Sphinx, push bishops down
in chilly chapels, a wafer in their mouths,
old men cry out his passage through their bowels.

3

No, no.
No word, none of these, no name, "Red Worm! Snake!"
What name makes him leave his hiding place?
Out of the null and void,
no name and no meaning: God, Yahweh, the Lord,
not to be spoken to, he never said a word
or took the power of death: the inconspicuous
plunge from air into sea he gave to us,
winds that wear away our towns . . . Who breathes
comes to nothing: absence, a world.

WALKING

I

His stride is part delusion.
They laugh at him, "A little water in the boot,
he thinks he walks on water."
At home to get a cup of coffee
he walks across Norway, and his talk—
sometimes he speaks intimately to crowds,
and to one person as to a crowd. On principle
he never eats small potatoes.
Illusion, mirage, hallucination,
he loves a night painting of a fable: a man
is grinning at a boy lighting a candle from an ember,
a monkey on his shoulder chained to heaven,—
a reminder that art apes nature.
When they told him "reality is simply what is,"
it was as though he had climbed Sinai,
then walked down to get the laws.
He dreams only of the migrations of peoples
beneath the migrations of birds,
he wakes to new nations, he yawns
riddles of the north and south wind,
whistles his own tune in the Holy Sepulchre.
Some afternoons he stretches out in a field
like an aqueduct, "All we do," he says,
"is carry a bucket or two of God's waters
from place to place."

2

Under a roof, and in the open air,
hangs an amusing tragedy, a kind of satyr play,
where not every fat man dancing by
is wrapped in grape leaves. Facing himself
in a bronze mirror like the one
the ancient Chinese thought cured insanity,

tongue-tied he speaks to his own secret face,
or standing in the sunlight
against the lives of mountains, sky and sea,
he speaks, made-up and masked, the lyrical truth,
the barefaced lie.
Not speaking the language of his fathers,
a hero may die because all flesh is grass
and he forgets the password.

From a lectern, or the top of a hay wagon,
or leaping down,
a few steps away from everyday life,
into something like a kitchen garden,
he unearths in the wordless soil
things sung or said, kinds of meaning:
what is denoted or symbolic,
or understood only by its music,
or caught onto without reason,
the endless twisting of its roots, its clarity.
He points to the old meaning of looking
to the Last Judgment,
while he believes nothing is merely or only.

              3

At a garden party he almost said,
"Madame, it is not in the bones of a lover or a dog
to wait long as the bleached mollusk
on the mountain. Time is an ice cube melting
in a bowl, the world is refracted, ridiculous.
In life, you often reach out for a stone
that isn't where you see it in the stream."
But it was summer,
no one would believe time was so cold
on a hot day, so comforting,
when the purple iris was already dry
and the tulips fallen.

5
Diary of a Satyr

WHEN I WAS A CHILD, I moved my pillow to a different part of the bed each night because I liked the feeling of not knowing where I was when I woke up. From the beginning I yearned for the nomadic life. I wandered, grazed like a goat on a hill—the move from grazing to exploring was just a leap over a fence. In my seventh year, I had a revelation. A teacher asked me a question. I knew the answer. Miss Green, a horse-faced redhead, asked the 3A class of P.S. 99, Kew Gardens, Queens, a long way from Byzantium: "What are you going to do in life?" Most of the answers remain a blur, but someone said she was going to be a novelist and someone said he'd write a play, or for the movies. I remember waiting; I was last to answer: "I am certain I am a poet." Then Miss Green said, "I knew it. You, Stanley, are a bronze satyr," and she whacked my erect penis with a twelve-inch Board of Education wooden ruler.

I ran home in a fury at my parents. They had never told me I was a satyr. My mother's explanation: "You know what a hard time I had giving birth to you. Why do you think every time I hit you it hurts my hand? You had whooping cough the first six months of your life. The doctor said no human being could survive that. Even so, when you were three months old in your crib, you knocked your five-year-old sister unconscious. Nothing ever fits you, not your shoes, not your pants, not your shirts, nothing. Your feet always hang off the bed." How many times did I hear my mother say, "That kid doesn't know his own strength. You'll injure somebody for life. Don't hit. Don't hit. The other kids, gentile and Jew, lie. You are mythological."

After the revelation, at dinner, I saw my father—a public high school principal—as an angry centaur. Most evenings he was out herding his mares and women together for song, smell, and conversation. At our dinner table, I knew if I didn't speak, no one would. My fifth summer, my father went to Europe "alone," mostly, I think, to Venice and Vienna. By watching others, I taught myself to swim. When he returned I couldn't look him in the eye. He brought back presents: a wooden bowl that, when lifted, played a Viennese waltz, a bronze ashtray of a boy peeing, after the fountain in Brussels, a silver top on a plunger I could never figure out, a blue necklace for my mother, some etchings of Venetian views and one of Beethoven. We lived in an apartment as desolate as Beethoven's jaw.

Still, on February 7, 1935, with my father on sabbatical leave, we set out as a family aboard the S.S. Statendam, heading for the stormy waters of the Atlantic, then southeast to the sunny Mediterranean. It was the first of many voyages I would take under different circumstances from the moral north to the warm south. For the first time, I heard the Roman languages of satyrs and satires, then Greek, Hebrew, Arabic, and Turkish. I heard rolling r's, strange j's and h's, sometimes silent, throated on olives, anchovies and garlic. Until that February, I had entered a house of worship only on special occasions—a Protestant Adirondack church in summer, to attend films—a synagogue, only once, to tell my grandmother on Yom Kippur that my mother was waiting outside in a car—I was thrown out for not wearing a hat, or perhaps because I was a satyr. My mother offered me hers, a brown, broad-brimmed hat with a veil that I refused to wear. Within a month, this satyr stood before the "Nightwatch" in Amsterdam. I read "Franco Franco Franco" on a wall in Malaga, I rode a camel beside the Sphinx, toured the Basilica of San Marco in Venice, watched men praying at the wailing wall; I entered the Church of the Nativity and the Holy Sepulcher, heard the "good news" for the first time. I took off my shoes, heard my hooves echo on the green rugs and tiles in the mosque of Santa Sophia and the Blue Mosque. I was photographed with the caryatids on the Acropolis, ran through the Parthenon on a windy February or March day, the Greek sun so bright against the white marble it hurt my eyes.

A few days later, on the Island of Rhodes, I was proud to be nicked in the leg by a ricocheted bullet in a post-revolutionary celebration. When I told the story throughout my childhood, I was shot in the leg in a Greek Revolution; I said I had a scar to prove it—and I do. That spring, I wandered off alone into the red light district of Algiers. An auburn-haired, tattooed lady smelling of flowers and sweat kissed me for nothing behind a beaded curtain. She touched a naked breast to my lips—I was in paradise. My mother thought I was lost. Soon, in Cairo, late at night, I roused most of the hotel attendants, claiming I had leprosy. I was covered with volcanoes of blood, my only comfort a black dragoman, tribal scars on his face, until my parents returned from a performance of belly dancers and made the discovery that I had been bitten by an army of fire ants. I would not forget the poverty and disease in the slums of Cairo, the crack of whips over the donkeys and horses. I was nine years old, eight years younger than the Soviet Union, changed forever.

Aboard the Statendam, I played chess with a thirteen-yearold kid named Matthew. He wore white knickers and traveled with his grandmother. I last saw him crying, kicking and spitting at my father, who was beating the dickens out of him. I never, in the two-month voyage, saw Matthew or his grandmother again. I asked my mother if Dad threw them overboard; she said, "You're exaggerating again." My father said, "To ask questions is a sign of intelligence, but you ask too many questions. Your mother is the Tower of Babel. You and she are two of a kind."

Now that I could accept and was proud of being a bronze satyr, I remembered when I was a baby in my Aunt Bessie's arms, I took her breasts out of her blouse, thinking, "I am pretending to be just a baby, but I am really out for a feel." I wish I had been photographed, then with my little victorious, evil satyr smile, instead of the family photo of me in a baby carriage reaching for a cloud. In our family, the beginning of civilization was understood to be the moment Abraham sacrificed the ram instead of his firstborn son. I started one dinner's conversation with "I think it would have been better to kill Isaac than the ram. I think the ram stands for me. Daddy, you know there's a very thin line between the good shepherd and the butcher."

"Who are you to think!" Whack went my father's Board of Education ruler, a thirty-six-inch weapon. My mother threatened to stab herself in the heart with a kitchen knife like a bronze

Lucretia. We were a family of atheists; still, we celebrated an occasional seder with uncles, aunts, and their children, most of whom kept away from me, lest I molest them. What could I do to liven up the evening? I planted a snail and a skeleton of an eel under the parsley and horseradish on my father's seder plate. The moment he passed out the horseradish, everyone saw the snail and eel's skeleton. I said, "Horseradish rhymes with Kaddish." Lightning, my father reached out for me, but he missed. I was ordered out of the house, into the world of wild things.

I had planned one last, beautiful gesture. My mother and Aunt Mabel had a friendly contest, who could make the lightest matzo balls. My mother always lost. I had found my aunt's matzo balls laid out on a platter in the kitchen. I took our little collection of stones and jewels from Jerusalem, and one by one I thrust them into the center of each matzo ball: diorite, opal, quartz, limestone, sandstone, onyx. I watched through the window as the matzo balls were served with a spoon, one by one, into the chicken soup. My aunt had a big and loyal constituency that typically gulped their food. Hypocrites, they swallowed the matzo balls with such comments as, "Light as air!" "Like perfume," until my cousin Audrey cried "I broke a tooth on a rock!" I danced my little goat dance outside for joy. For the first and only time in her life, my dear mother was declared a winner.

Whatever the weather, the smoke of battle never cleared. In November, on the anniversary of my grandfather's death, my mother lit a Yartzheit memorial candle in a glass. I believe she prayed. "What would happen," I asked, "if I blew out the flame?" My mother's face saddened that I should ask such an unspeakable question, but she knew my ways. "That would be a sin." She almost never used that word. Now I knew there was a second sin—the first, the greater sin, wasting food. A proper satyr, sin was my pie in the sky. I knew that in one evening Alcibiades had cut the penises off half the herms in Athens. I scouted the neighborhood, and in one evening, with our nineteenth-century American candle-snuffer, I put out the flames of seven Yartzheit candles. I came across a magazine called *Twice a Year* that introduced me to Rimbaud, Lorca, Wallace Stevens; they taught me how to survive. Out of a bar of Ivory soap I carved a Virgin Mother with a baby satyr in her lap, then another virgin with a unicorn in her lap. My thought was the unicorn represented, not Christ, but my savior— poetry. I cut school and went two or three days a week to the main reading room of the Forty-Second Street Library (a satyr among lions), or the Museum of Modern Art, or to the Apollo Theater to see foreign films. I smoked five-cent Headline cigars. One romantic evening I called my father a sadist (the first shot of the fourth Punic War). It was then I was banished from Jackson Heights forever.

Hard years. I learned to disguise myself to earn a living. Wherever I went I carried my desperately thin production of poems and Wallace Stevens. I was sure Hitler was anti-satyr. I joined the Navy at seventeen. A sword wound and the G.I. Bill got me through college in style. I had a recurring nightmare that, like the satyr Marsyus, I was flayed—just for being a satyr, for no reason at all, not for challenging Apollo at music. I leapt around graduate women's dorms, broke windows and doors. Police were called. I was expelled for "subversive activity." Now history: I was hired by a detective agency to spy on organizing workers. I became a counterspy for Local 65. I sang in a band, played the bass, waited on tables; I was a sailor on a Greek merchant ship (I got the job through Rae Dalven, the translator of Cavafy); I grazed a while at New Directions; for mysterious reasons, Dylan Thomas and I became passionate friends—I loved his poetry and his deep-throated Christianity. I remember his saying "the truth doesn't hurt." He could and would talk intimately to anyone, regardless of class or education, not a habit of American or English intellectuals. He drank, he told me, because he wasn't useful, which I understood to mean he could not relieve human suffering. Anyone who really cared about him knew how profoundly and simply Christian he was. Dickens was a favorite teacher. He gave away the shirt off his back. The turtleneck sweater Dylan wore in that picture was mine, knitted for me by my Aunt Tilly. We discovered an Italian funeral home on Bleecker Street where, after the bars closed at 4 a.m., we drank whiskey on a gold and onyx coffin. He introduced me to Theodore Roethke, his second-favorite living American poet. His favorite was e.e. cummings—"he can write about anything." Dylan, Ted and I spent an evening with townspeople from Laugharne, trolls who whitewashed the town. What a concert of Welsh accents and laughter. Dylan had his boathouse, Roethke his greenhouse, I had my apartment house in Queens.

I met a blond, green-eyed Catalan beauty named Ana Maria. Full of Spanish poetry and Catalan republican-heretical-anarchistic tragedy, she was a great bad-weather friend. After Barnard College she sailed off to Spain; I followed, after writing a poem called "Sailing from the United States." (I earned the money to follow by wild luck—an old Eighth Street satyr who knew I loved painting gave me an El Greco to sell, a crucifixion with a view of Toledo.) We married at the American Consulate in Tangiers. Our witnesses—her mother and two virgin sisters. There was blood on the floor. It turned out that one of her sisters had been given a metal garter with nails by a nun at the Colegio del Sagrado Corazón because the nun thought Ana Maria was marrying an American Protestant. A miracle: the sister who wore the garter and shed her blood at my wedding found her way to Philadelphia, married an orthodox Jew, a painter. They both died too soon and are buried on a hillside overlooking Haifa.

I knew in Rome there was a tradition of centaur teachers— why not satyrs? I made my way to pagan Rome. I taught English and tutored. We lived facing the temple of the Vestal Virgins across the Tiber. I decided, one August evening, to have a mythological picnic, a cookout for my mythological friends. Of course, it had to be beside the river, on the embankment of the Tiber, because the hippocamps were half-horse, half-fish; the tritons were half-man, half-fish. There were nymphs and maenads. The great god Pan himself came—and the Artemis of Ephesus on a sacred barge. (You understand I could not serve my famous fish soup.) A giraffe crashed the party. He said he was a tree, a sycamore among men, lonely since his nesting birds flew south. He said he envied trees that can lean over a river and see their reflection. Madness I thought, to have a private mythology, but I knew to speak to him I had to accept his metaphor. The symposium began. How did it feel to a man to make love to a fish, how did it feel to a horse to make love to a fish? What was love? Someone complimented Artemis on the beauty of her many breasts. A harpy screeched, "She has no nipples; they are the testicles of sacrificed bulls." We all came out of darkness, hatched from a single egg that was love the enchanting, the brilliant. When we departed, we kissed goodbye in our several heartfelt ways. Some wept because the sirens, as usual, sang their song of how we would be remembered.

I spent years in Rome, happy to eat the leftovers of the gods, reading and writing, trying to make a living holding four jobs simultaneously. More than once, drunk on Frascati, I bathed in the Bernini fountain of the four rivers. On summer evenings, I drank from the Nile with a marble tiger. I corresponded with my mother. I received one letter from my father I carried around a while. Finally I destroyed it, lest God should see it. Out of the blue, I received a postcard from my father, "We will be in Pisa on August 18, 1956, at the Hotel Cavellieri, if you care to see us." Signed, "Pop." Never, not once in my life, did I call my father "Pop." I arrived on the appointed day, shocked to see how much they had aged. They were fifty-eight. We had lunch in the piazza, the pages of the Bible flapping in the wind. A little peeved that I had learned Italian and Spanish in the passing years, my father taught himself passing Italian and Spanish to go with his Greek, Latin, and French. He had more than enough Italian to order, as usual, exactly what he wanted. He insisted on having his spaghetti with cinnamon and sugar, no doubt a Litvak recipe out of his mother's kitchen. My mother said my hair was getting straight; did that have anything to do with the Leaning Tower of Pisa? Oh, how I miss my mother's questions. My father spent a cordial week in Italy, my mother another month at our apartment in Trastevere. She slept in a room I usually rented out, in a bed just vacated by Christopher Isherwood and friend. If she had known, would she have slept a wink? My father said, in wishing me goodbye, "If you had only been a bronze horse rearing up once in a while, I could have handled you." What was our mettle, a word I misspelled in my head as m-e-t-a-l? What we were really made of, the years would prove.

Coming out of his thoughts, my father said abruptly, "What I know of poetry I owe to you."

"How so?" I asked suspiciously.

"When I was studying for my principal's exam when you were two or three, I had to memorize passages from Shakespeare.

On walks, I would recite the great speeches over your head, and repeat them out loud until I had them: *Hamlet, King Lear, The Tempest.*"

I said, "Perhaps what I know of poetry I owe to you."

He started reciting "O, what a rogue and peasant slave am I" with his large, tin ear. I finished it. I kissed him and said, "Thanks a lot." (A well-known actress from a famous acting family once put me down with "I saw my father play King Lear when I was ten. You couldn't possibly understand the difference between that and studying Shakespeare at Yale." I informed her that I began my Shakespeare studies when I was two.)

I met Ted Roethke again in Rome when I was a hired hoof on the review *Botteghe Oscure.* We both had passed dangers. We hit it off. We met again two years later by chance at a Pinter play in London when I was heading back to the States after Rome fell. We joined up to see *Hamlet* and Gielgud in *The Tempest* (we did not drown our books). Eight seasons passed. Ted and Beatrice came to stay with me at Fifty-Seventh Street at a barn I was living in. I gave Ted big breakfasts and my homburg, he gave me his famous raccoon skin coat. He liked my fish and turtle tank in my small dining room. He told me he was once in love with a snake. Ted brought me to dinner at Stanley Kunitz's. I remember that first long, long, long evening. Thinking back, I didn't quite know how lucky I was. They were in their fifties, Stanley had almost fifty years to go, Ted had six. Dylan had crossed the Styx a handful of years before. On still another evening, not after death, Roethke came with his not-quite-finished manuscript of *The Far Field.* He went off one evening to show it to Stanley Kunitz. He put on a blue serge suit and my homburg for the occasion. Just before dawn, he rolled back in. "What did Stanley say?" I asked.

"He liked it a lot." Then a look of pain crossed his face and I knew that Ted, who had been in the mood to be crowned heavy-weight champion and nothing less, was disheartened. I thought Kunitz had found something not quite right, that he had been demanding and not just celebratory. Suddenly, Ted said, talking half to me and half to the world, "Stanley Kunitz is the most honest man in America." I told this story in an introduction to a book of Kunitz conversations. More years. Roethke long dead, after a formal Roethke celebration at which Kunitz, an aged ex-Roethke sweetheart and I were the only three people in the room who knew him, Kunitz asked me to repeat the story at dinner to a young poet. I was pleased my story had touched Stanley.

My mother divorced my father six months before her death. On her birthday, a month to the day before she died, she saw her second great-granddaughter, who, to her joy, was named after her. She never knew she had a grandson. My sister sent our mother's ashes through the U.S. mail. My parents are buried in a garden I made in Water Mill, the graves two unmarked stones, surrounded by Montauk daisies and pink mallow. I didn't think my mother would want the stones too close. Last spring, a swan nested right on the graves. When the eggs hatched, the mother swan paraded with her six grey cygnets in the bay in front of our house. When I approached, they all jumped on their mother's back, and she swam away with them to safety. My mother would have liked that.

INDEX OF TITLES